HAND-GRENADE PRACTICE IN PEKING

Hand-Grenade Practice in Peking

My part in the
Cultural Revolution

FRANCES WOOD

JOHN MURRAY
Albemarle Street, London

© Frances Wood 2000

First published in 2000
by John Murray (Publishers) Ltd,
50 Albemarle Street, London W1X 4BD

The moral right of the author has been asserted

A catalogue record for this book is available from the British Library

ISBN 0-7195-5781 X

Typeset in 12/14 Garamond by Servis Filmsetting Ltd, Manchester
Printed and bound in Great Britain by The University Press, Cambridge

To everyone who was there,
including those from whom I have
borrowed and those I have erased
or conflated, with thanks for
helping me to endure

Contents

Illustrations

The illustrations are taken from *Huang Jiguang: aiguozhuyi he guojizhuyi de yangbang* (*Huang Jiguang: A Model of Patriotism and Internationalism*, Shanghai, 1970), purchased by me as light reading matter at the Jinggangshan revolutionary base area in 1971. Huang Jiguang was born into a poor peasant family in 1930 and, if the illustrations are to be believed, spent his early life looking determined, especially when facing up to the local evil landlord and plotting revenge. After Liberation, he joined the People's Liberation Army and, according to the book, during the Korean War 'threw himself at the enemy firing point, using his own bosom to block the enemy's machine gun'. Looking up the 'block' character in a modern dictionary, I discovered that the second gloss on the character is a slight variant. 'Defying death, Huang Jiguang threw himself against the embrasure of the enemy's blockhouse.' It must be presumed that he was killed, although the book is unaccountably coy about his end. Young models of patriotism and internationalism do not die, they simply acquire a background of red flags.

The Cultural Revolution

While I was studying Chinese at Cambridge from 1968 to 1971, China was closed to the outside world. The country was in the throes of the Cultural Revolution, though the only evidence of the widespread violence that accompanied it was the number of bodies found floating in the Pearl River near Hong Kong and Macao, the savage rhetoric of the *People's Daily* and, in London, the vision of Chinese diplomats threatening the police with capitalist baseball bats outside their embassy in Portland Place. Learning Chinese then was like learning a dead language: there seemed no hope of ever using it in China. The closest we were likely to get was the island of Taiwan, and all our language work was geared to Taiwanese usage which preserved much politesse temporarily abandoned by the comrades on the mainland.

Although it is now said to have lasted from 1966 to 1976 (and is retrospectively described in today's China as 'the ten disastrous years'), the origins of the (once) Great Proletarian Cultural Revolution lay in earlier disagreements within the Chinese Communist Party. Mao Zedong's rise to power within the Party from 1919 had involved a series of long and bitter fights with 'right-deviationists' and 'left-splittists'. These were officially known in China as the heroic Ten Great Struggles and were explained as 'line struggles', or disagreements over the correct political line, rather than personal battles in which Mao eliminated all opposition.

Soon after the establishment of the People's Republic of China in 1949, Mao, now supreme leader, initiated a further series of campaigns to eradicate any remaining opposition, both within the upper ranks of the Party and outside it. Some of these were cunning plans, like the Hundred Flowers movement of 1956 in which Zhou Enlai* encouraged intellectuals to make helpful suggestions as to how the nation might be better governed under the slogan 'Let a hundred flowers blossom, let a hundred schools of thought contend'. Those who were foolish enough to open their mouths found themselves condemned in the subsequent Anti-Rightist movement of 1957 and sent, often for years, to the countryside for 're-education' from the masses.

There was also disagreement within the Chinese Communist Party between those who supported a Communist bloc and recognized the leadership of the Soviet Union as the senior Communist state, and Mao who was scornful of Soviet achievements and opposed emulation of Soviet practice, particularly in the countryside. The Great Leap Forward of 1958 was Mao's attempt to sinicize Communism, turning away from Soviet-style concentration on heavy industry. Instead he proposed that agriculture be

---

* Zhou Enlai (1898–1976) was a well-born and well-educated Communist leader who fronted most of China's post-1949 diplomatic endeavours, charming all he met. There must, nevertheless, have been steel behind the charm, for he managed for nearly fifty years to maintain a prominent position within the Communist Party without ever, apparently, provoking Mao's jealousy. One reason for this may have been his reluctance to assume the position of 'heir apparent', preferring to be only third in line, thus avoiding the inevitable fate of all Mao's designated successors.

more fully socialized, with industrialization of the country-side and the formation of large agricultural units, called the People's Communes.

The industrialization of the countryside involved the establishment of 'backyard furnaces' in which the peasants were supposed to produce pig-iron. There were significant achievements from this attempt to integrate agriculture and industry: China pioneered successful treatments for severe burns and complex limb reconstruction through the resultant accidents. Mao, meanwhile, announced with unconscious irony that 'Stalin has only one leg [heavy industry] but we have two legs [socialized agriculture and backyard industry].'

Though there had been earlier, village- and family-based efforts to collectivize agriculture, the establishment of the People's Communes gave the state far greater control over production. In addition, agricultural labour could now be mobilized in the slack season to work on necessary infrastructural improvements such as the building of roads, canals and dams. But the political impetus behind the creation of the People's Communes led to dreadful problems. Mao insisted on the use of various slogans to increase crop yields. They worked as sound-bites but were disastrous in practice. They included 'close planting' to produce dense crops which, as any gardener could have foretold, only led to the death of a vast number of seedlings. 'Deep ploughing', a favourite agricultural slogan of Josef Stalin, himself no *kulak*, meant that farmers had to work harder than ever to dig ridiculously deep furrows: whether this had any effect on productivity was never successfully demonstrated but it exhausted the peasants. Pest control was carried out under the banner of eradicating the 'four evils': birds, rats, insects and flies. Between 1958 and 1960, millions of small birds died of exhaustion as peasants and city-dwellers banged drums and saucepan lids day and night to prevent them from perching anywhere. By 1960, it was realized that the dearth of birds was making the elimination of flies and other insects an impossible task, and birds were removed from the list of evils.

This political transformation of agriculture encouraged a misplaced enthusiasm amongst provincial leaders for reporting bumper harvests. Eager to fulfil Mao's Utopian vision they artificially inflated production figures, and photographs of great piles of wheat or dense fields of rice were faked. In fact the peasants were starving. Between 1958 and 1961, there was a famine so widespread that at least 30 million people died.

In late 1958, Mao voluntarily stepped down as Chairman of the Communist Party, ostensibly to 'study' but effectively leaving his designated successors to face the disastrous consequences of his policies. In his years away from the centre of power, he became increasingly convinced that the new leadership was becoming bourgeois and corrupt, and that the people had lost touch with revolutionary struggle. He became determined to continue his revolution by eradicating 'bourgeois' opposition and transforming society through the reform of 'culture'. In Marxist terms 'culture' is defined as not just the arts but the entire institutional superstructure of society. Thus all government and educational organizations, as well as 'culture' in the narrower definition, required attention.

In late 1965, a campaign against a play opened the Great Proletarian Cultural Revolution. The play had been written four years earlier by Wu Han, China's foremost historian and a liberal politician who had served briefly as Mayor of Peking. Entitled *Hai Rui xia guan* (*Hai Rui Dismissed from*

Office), its hero was an honest official of the Ming dynasty (1368–1644) whose defence of the legitimate grievances of local peasants had provoked the Emperor to dismiss him. Wu Han was referring indirectly to local officials who during the famine had tried to alert the Communist Party to falsified figures, pointing out that inaccurate harvest returns would not help the central government. The attack on Wu Han by the Party's propaganda department signalled the beginning of an onslaught on the whole field of culture in China.

Using slogans such as 'Bombard the Headquarters', Mao bounced back to power, encouraging young people to create their own revolution. Huge rallies of young students massed in Tiananmen Square in the centre of Peking, hysterically waving plastic-covered copies of 'The Little Red Book', a collection of quotations from Mao's writings that had been produced so that activists could select the appropriate slogan without too much effort. These young Red Guard students and schoolchildren seized control in China's cities and set about correcting the existing leadership.

Everyone was encouraged to participate whether in a primary school, a hospital or a factory. Anyone in a position of power was automatically attacked through gruelling 'struggle sessions' in which they were made to wear dunce's hats and to submit to screamed accusations and, often, physical violence from their fellow-workers. If they survived the struggle sessions (and many were killed or driven to suicide), they were sentenced to reform their ideology through unpleasant tasks. There was a strongly lavatorial aspect to reform through labour: brain surgeons were made to clean lavatories by hand, professors of literature were set to look after pigs, and much manure was moved about. Whole offices, from ministries to university administrations, from departments of museum curators to faculties of professors, were 'sent to the countryside' for periods of months or even years to learn the dignity of labour from the peasants.

Families were torn apart as parents vanished to the countryside. Many young children were left behind to manage as best they could. Daily life became dangerous when Red Guard groups fought amongst themselves on ideological grounds. Essential shopping expeditions became terrifying if they involved crossing various Red Guard barricades. In

1968, partly to remove some of these young urban terrorists, Mao ordered that all young people should also go to the countryside to learn from the peasants. Eventually he even turned on the student activists of Peking University who had been at the forefront of the movement, and political control was gradually shifted to a new triumvirate of 'workers, peasants and soldiers'. The army was brought into the cities to re-establish control and by 1972 a new order was imposed.

All institutions were to be run by Revolutionary Committees composed of another heroic triad, this time of workers, peasants and Party members.

As the Cultural Revolution progressed, Mao's wife, Jiang Qing, who in her youth had been a fairly unsuccessful film actress in Shanghai, took the opportunity to eradicate her old enemies in the (more narrowly defined) cultural field. She was also closely associated with the promotion of truly proletarian culture in the form of ten 'acceptable' Peking operas, among them *The Red Lantern, The Red Detachment of Women* and *Taking Tiger Mountain by Strategy*, and the ballet *The White-haired Girl*, that dominated China's stages for ten years. Western music was condemned because it was, inevitably, foreign in origin and bourgeois in inspiration. Debussy was decadent, Chopin neurotic and even Beethoven (good in parts, what with *Fidelio*) had made the mistake of writing both the religious *Missa Solemnis* and a symphony in praise of a tyrant.

Beyond the factional politics and Madam Mao's pursuit of presumed enemies, there was a massive attempt to change people's lives and attitudes, to create a new socialist person. All sorts of bourgeois pleasures were banned. The cinema and the theatre were dominated by Madam Mao's politically correct productions. Paintings of flowers or, worse, nudes, were condemned and destroyed in favour of political pictures showing red flags and tractors amongst neatly planted fields or heroic depictions of scenes in the life of Chairman Mao, with heartening titles like *Chairman Mao Is Here on Our Battleship*. Ballroom dancing was outlawed and, though Mao had reputedly said in 1958, 'Let's be pretty', all forms of personal adornment and decoration were eliminated. Women could no longer perm their hair or dress to attract. Those who did so were dragged through the streets and had their hair clipped or their tight trousers ripped in public by Red Guards with straight, short hair and baggy trousers.

All museums were closed, apparently on the orders of Zhou Enlai who wanted to protect their ancient and therefore reprehensible contents. Most of the major temples were similarly shut, to protect them from Red Guards intent upon destroying the 'old society'. There was, in the end, surprisingly little damage done to historic monuments as a result of this pre-emptive move. Red Guards were also occasionally lazy. They did storm the Buddhist holy island of Putuoshan, off the coast south of Shanghai, but Jiuhuashan, another Buddhist mountain deep in Anhui province, was spared. Though its temples and pagodas had been devastated by the Taiping uprising in 1851–7, the mountain's relative inaccessibility protected it from the Cultural Revolution. The monks, anxiously listening to the radio, retreated to the top of the mountain and waited. After seven years and no sign of any Red Guards, they came down again.

The worst destruction was probably inflicted on family property. When the Red Guards came calling, they ransacked houses, destroying documents, letters, photographs and old furniture. Many families, fearful that possessions such as old books, foreign books, diaries and letters might constitute counter-revolutionary matter, burnt them themselves. Anything connected with the polluted outside world or with wicked pre-revolutionary China represented a danger. Precious textbooks and scholarly notes might be seen as indications of a hankering after prestige, setting their possessors apart from the mass.

All forms of expertise were denigrated in favour of peasant wisdom and all forms of private ownership were abolished. Peasants were forced to work only for the commune and, in the most 'advanced' rural brigades, a sort of collective life was enforced, with communal kitchens and communal child-care. Various 'models' were held up for emulation. The revolutionary production brigade at Dazhai, in the poor north-western province of Shanxi, was hailed as the acme of ideological motivation. Its inhabitants, though poor, were apparently delighted with their fully communal life. The new socialist person cared only for the commune and was prepared to sacrifice his or her family and even life itself for the collective good.

For many, particularly those who had developed any form of expertise, often with the most patriotic of intentions, this was a tragic time. Many were killed. Famous pianists had their fingers broken by Red Guards, famous novelists were tortured and committed suicide. Hundreds of thousands of intellectuals were imprisoned in the most primitive conditions or forced to join labour brigades in the frozen north. The effect on their families spread beyond the death or imprisonment of the individual concerned. The children of such prominent figures, already bereft, were forbidden to go to university and were disbarred from any normal activities. Some were unable to bear the pressure.

After 1971 when the army, on Mao's orders, re-established control, life returned to a new sort of normality, with 'politics in command'. The universities reopened, after a fashion. They only admitted 'worker-peasant-soldier students' and then only after applicants had spent at least two years in the countryside or working in a factory. There were no entrance exams. In fact there were no exams of any kind – Mao had condemned them as 'surprise attacks' and recommended cheating. Instead it was the potential students' political attitude that counted.

Though most of its intellectuals and many bureaucrats were still enduring forced manual labour in the countryside, in the early Seventies China began to open up a little to the outside world. Tourism was resumed, although only on a small and highly political scale, restricted at first to members of Maoist Friendship Associations from all over the world who, rather than seeing ancient sites or museums, visited tractor factories and irrigation schemes and listened to long accounts of the Cultural Revolution and its achievements. In the summer of 1971, just after I graduated, I was lucky to be included in the first British revolutionary 'young persons' delegation' to visit China since 1966. My fellow-delegates were mainly very left-wing students, with the odd worker, and I scraped into the group through my knowledge of the language. The trip was relentlessly political and mainly consisted of sitting in hot steamy rooms being introduced to the members of hundreds of revolutionary committees and hearing interminable accounts of the progress and achievements of the Cultural Revolution in that particular city, factory, hospital, primary school or agricultural commune.

In every city I asked about the local museum. Every museum was still closed. But if the trip was culturally disappointing, it had its compensations. For the first time I could actually talk to Chinese people, even if I did make all sorts of mistakes. When asked by a nervous group of peasants who shuffled quietly after me in their cloth shoes, 'Have you eaten?' – the Chinese equivalent of 'How are you?' which only requires a yes or a no – I gave them a plate-by-plate account of my lunch. Even so, it was wonderful to be able to wander through a village street and to see soft blue-green lotus leaves growing in bright green ricefields, little boys riding on the back of water buffaloes or herding ducks and an old peasant in a straw raincoat who looked as though he'd stepped out of a Chinese painting.

Like pain, the memory of the boredom of much of my visit in 1971, and of those interminable meetings with revolutionary committees, faded with time and in 1975 I applied to join the third group of British exchange students to go and study for a year in Peking. Though I could read Chinese and had a good job in a university library, working with Chinese books, I wanted to speak the language better. What follows is an account, based on letters home, of my year in China. To all those who suffered terribly at the time I apologize for my determination to amuse myself and be amused by what I found. 1 only began to discover what was happening to China's intellectuals when I got back home.

Model Revolutionary Life

On 25 September 1975, ten British students, selected and supported by the British Council, boarded an Ilyushin plane in Hong Kong. Rose was studying Chinese art history and archaeology at London. Beth, who had just graduated from Cambridge, had more reason than the rest of us for worry as she had left her husband and dog behind for a year. There was a large contingent from Leeds University. Among them, Gerry and Jim had also graduated whilst Sarah, small and seeming terribly young, had just finished her second year.*

On the flight to Peking we were served sweets, Chinese chewing-gum (very intractable) and cigarettes by very young stewardesses wearing ancient calico shirts. Silenced by the thought that we had left the familiar behind for a whole year, we landed at Peking airport in the dark. A tiny man called Fu Laoshi, wearing pebble glasses, an incredibly wide smile and

* Rose is now Head of the Far East Department at the Victoria and Albert Museum and an esteemed ceramic historian. Beth is the Curator of Korean collections at the British Library. The rest have become diplomats, aid workers, museum directors or lecturers, or are involved in business.

a grey peaked cap, led us with our voluminous luggage to an ancient coach and we drove through the dark, silent countryside for about an hour. Our destination was the Foreign Languages Institute.

The coach stopped outside a grey brick building and the girls were unloaded and ushered, in pairs, into small rooms with bare whitewashed walls on the second floor. I soon discovered that all Chinese rooms were similarly whitewashed and that if you brushed against a wall the white came off on your clothes. My room, solely mine for the time being owing to odd numbers, contained two iron beds, one wooden bookshelf, two desks and two chairs. A single lightbulb dangled from the ceiling. The windows were bare of curtains and the door had no lock but had to be fastened from outside by a padlock, not provided by the management. The management did issue (against multiple signatures on flimsy paper chits) an enamel washing-basin (plain), a thermos flask (made of red tin with huge blowsy roses painted on the side), a single, very hard pillow with pillow-case, a single sheet and a large, heavy quilt made of thick cotton wadding, covered with yellow cotton dotted with tiny flowers and with a white cotton sheet sewn on to the bottom.

The washing-basin was for use in the second-floor washroom which had a row of taps over a long grey concrete trough. The taps produced cold water, except for a rush-hour period of two hours every evening between seven and nine when there was hot water, also available in the showers on the ground floor. Next to the showers was an enormous boiler dotted with terrifying dials, their red needles always pointing at temperatures which indicated imminent explosion. Boiling steam issued from various cracks in the pipework but this machine was central to life. Here we filled our thermoses in order to wash in warm water in the mornings and here we would find a supply of safe drinking-water.

Next morning, as the sun streamed in through the uncurtained window, the Foreign Languages Institute was revealed. Tall dusty grey-brick buildings stretched away into the distance ahead; to the left was a huge open expanse, equally dusty and presumably a sports ground. On it Chinese students in plain white shirts and baggy cotton trousers of either dark blue or greenish khaki were wandering about carrying textbooks from which they were apparently memorizing texts by reading them aloud.

The Foreign Languages Institute lay in the north-western corner of Peking, in an area surrounded by fields where most of the academic institutes were clustered, not far from Peking University. It took in foreign students from Europe (Albania, Romania, Yugoslavia, Italy, Spain, Denmark, Sweden, Norway, Iceland, France, Germany and Austria), Canada, Australia, New Zealand, all kinds of African countries and friendly Asian states including Japan, Cambodia, Laos and North Korea. All of us were there to study Chinese; and the African and Asian students were mostly doing so in order to pursue further studies in engineering or medicine in China. There was also a contingent of Chinese students who were studying foreign languages of all sorts.

The building immediately opposite the girls' block was the canteen and beyond it was the boys' dormitory. The canteen was divided into two parts. On one side was the Chinese section where for almost no money at all you could eat a great quantity of uninspiring food, but this was closed to us on our first morning because to eat there you had to bring your own bowls and spoons. In the Western section, Western breakfast was served and crockery was provided. Because of the (slightly) greater choice of food available and the provision of crockery, this was more expensive than the Chinese side.

After breakfast, we were collected by a minibus and taken to the British Embassy. Most embassies, including ours, were in the south-eastern part of the city, in a district called Jianguomen wai (Outside the Gate of the Establishment of the Nation), just to the east of the old Jesuit Observatory, a turreted grey-brick tower, closed to visitors like everything else, whose astrolabes, armillary spheres and sundial could be seen silhouetted against the sky above the battlements.

At the Embassy we were given a serious talk by the Head of Chancery about not getting into trouble. He also wanted us to list our next-of-kin in case we fell off our bicycles or worse. This was our first introduction to the slightly schizophrenic life of the foreign student in Peking. We were invited to join the Embassy Social Club for an annual fee of 10 yuan (about the equivalent of four months' breakfasts in the Chinese canteen) in order to be able to borrow books from the library, see films and use the Embassy pub, The Bell, where we could play darts and sign chitties for drinks (anything from beer to Campari and soda).

Next, the minibus took us to the Friendship Store, just around the corner from the British Embassy. Close to the Friendship Store were two large compounds guarded by People's Liberation Army soldiers with rifles and hand-guns. Here Embassy staff and their families lived in handsome flats with balconies. Their maids, cooks and *ayis* (nannies) were all provided by the Public Security Bureau and were universally assumed to be fluent linguists, graduates of Moscow's University of the Toilers of the East, who reported daily on significant exchanges over the marmalade and toast.

Embassy families did most of their shopping (for items that did not fit into the capacious diplomatic bag) in the

Friendship Store. On the ground floor were Chinese medi-
cines, a tiny stall selling flowers and goldfish, and food. I had
been most depressed at the thought of a cheese-less year but
that first morning I discovered that the Friendship Store
offered (stocks permitting) a sort of dry Edam cheese with a
pink wax rind, which was immensely cheering. There was
also bread: the white bread disappeared very early in the
morning but the little dark brown, Russian-influenced loaves
were very good. Butter was sold in tiny half packets as in

France and was slightly rancid but there was unbelievably
cheap caviare from the Amur available, so cheap in fact that
students could afford to eat it in huge quantities for Sunday
breakfast. *Petits-fours* that melted in the mouth were also dangerously low-priced – tiny cone-shaped wafers stuffed with
fondant chocolate, *petits sablés* in chocolate and vanilla che-
quer-board patterns, and miniature cream horns. As most of
what was 'foreign' in China then had come from Russia,

I wondered if the pastry-cooks had studied in Moscow at the feet of some reformed imperial chef.

Hugely encouraged by the familiar edibles in the Friendship Store and by the news that the very kind Embassy would send the minibus to collect us every Friday for an evening at The Bell, we were driven back to the Languages Institute across the vast expanse of Tiananmen Square. It was flanked to the east by the great grim building which housed the Museum of Chinese History. This was closed owing to comprehensive revisions in the official view of Chinese history. Opposite was the pillared portico of the Great Hall of the People where mysterious government meetings took place. To the distant south lay the great barbican Qianmen (Front Gate). The only construction within the vast square was the Monument to the People's Heroes, a tall grey stone obelisk with bas-reliefs around the base depicting glorious struggles such as the destruction of British and American opium in 1842, the demonstration against the Treaty of Versailles on 4 May 1919, another demonstration, this time against the Japanese and the British in Shanghai on 30 May 1925, and the production of 'grain for the front'. On either side were huge portraits of Marx, Engels and Lenin, all heavily bearded, and Stalin, mustachioed, each made of hundreds of glazed tiles. Set slightly apart was a similar tiled portrait of Sun Yat-sen, his facial arrangements hidden under a thicket of bamboo scaffolding erected for repairs. Portraiture in the square was completed with the painting of Chairman Mao which hung over the central gateway in the Gate of Heavenly Peace itself, the entrance to the imperial Forbidden City.

On our first Saturday in China, I rose virtuously at 6 a.m. in order to join a *taijiquan* class. *Taijiquan* (Supreme Fist) is an ancient form of exercise, sometimes translated as 'shadow boxing', in which you move slowly through a prescribed series of movements intended to harmonize your *qi* or cosmic breath. Outside on the sports field, an elderly gentleman with a shaved head and aristocratic manner led a class of stumbling foreigners. Chinese students, who disdained this traditional exercise as suitable only for reactionary old persons and foreigners, showed off on parallel bars, played football or wandered between us, ostentatiously reading the very politically correct journal *Hongqi* (*Red Flag*), the 'theoretical' organ of the People's Liberation Army.

After a Western breakfast of fried eggs and lightly charred bread, all English students were required to report for a medical examination. We had all had to have a medical in England and had arrived as instructed with chest X-rays but the Institute was not prepared to take the word of any foreign 'capitalist-roader' doctor without double-checking. We let the side down pretty badly. Two fainted (both men, of course), the second taking the table and most of the doctors with him. The interesting thing was that they had fainted before anything actually happened. Perhaps it was the peculiar smell of whatever the Chinese used as a disinfectant. It had such an effect on Gerry that ever after he had to make a huge detour around the medical centre lest he topple over again.

Unsystematically and unfairly, all the boys were allowed to miss out the needle bits and it was left to the females to provide vast donations of blood for unknown purposes. What with the delays, we were all let off our X-rays (indefinitely as it turned out) but we had hours of fun watching other foreign students having theirs. The X-ray machine was one of those screens where you walk past and everyone can see your entire skeleton in movement. I thought it was fascinating though the others said it looked like something straight out of *Cancer Ward* and that the doctor was doomed. As more foreign students filed in for their medicals, a crisis arose. A large group of very small Cambodians wearing Mao jackets and sarongs clearly knew no Chinese. The doctors knew no Cambodian. As my French was a lot better than my Chinese, I volunteered to stand decorously behind a screen, passing on instructions as best I could: *'Messieurs, enlevez vos jupes, s'il vous plaît!'*

In the afternoon we were introduced to our Friendship Class which consisted almost entirely of comfortable middle-aged Chinese who had suddenly been told to learn English in order to promote revolution. Such apparently arbitrary orders interfered often with the daily life of Chinese citizens. They couldn't refuse because this might suggest that they weren't prepared to make sacrifices. As it was, since Chairman Mao had said that they should fear neither hardship nor death for the sake of the revolution, they had had to leave their jobs and families and spend a year in the Languages Institute. With one exception, they did not appear to have been selected on the basis of linguistic talent because that would have run counter to the ethos of egalitarianism and hinted at the cultivation of 'expertise' which was a very dirty word in China at the time. Fortunately, most of them were from the Peking area and so could at least spend the weekends with their families. Not this weekend, however. Half a dozen sensible, middle-aged ladies were detailed to take us off to the nearest group of shops at Wudaokou (Crossroads No. 5), a village near the back gate of the Institute.

There, in the 'department store', a dimly lit shop that sold everything except vegetables, we purchased shallow enamel bowls and little speckled enamel spoons so that we could eat in the Chinese canteen. There was no need for chopsticks – canteen eating was all about shovelling. Not even the

Chinese students used them, although they did do so at home where they lived more graciously. On the street outside we also bought apples and small ready-peeled roasted chestnuts. We were very heavily chaperoned, probably as a result of all that fainting in the morning, but it was amusing to watch our classmate Mrs Zhao fiercely negotiating the purchase of beancurd from a huge wicker basket on the back of the vendor's bike and picking over vegetables with disdain before she went home to collect her son from his kindergarten. Owing to his mother's linguistic assignment he was a weekly boarder.

That evening there was an open-air film on the playing-field, for students and the local inhabitants. At the height of the Cultural Revolution, some five years earlier, the only acceptable cultural items had been the ten revolutionary Peking operas masterminded by Madam Mao. By the mid-Seventies, other cultural events were possible but this did not mean that they were any the less carefully controlled. Our first introduction to the Chinese cinema was *Haixia* (*Sea Mist*), a sort of Moses story about a baby found in a basket on the Fujian coast but which soon turned tragic as death piled on death. Miss Sea Mist's father and innumerable brothers, fearing neither hardship nor death in their efforts to feed the nation, drowned amidst violent storms. Her adopted mother died rather inexplicably of 'hardship' and her uncle was killed by evil Kuomintang soldiers in the pay of Chiang Kai-shek, based on the nearby island of Taiwan. Then the People's Liberation Army arrived and overcame Miss Sea Mist's natural suspicion of soldiers by washing up all the cups in sight and joining her in a frugal supper of grass and bark. From then on, everything was all right. We had taken out chairs as ordered but couldn't sit down as the entire village of Wudaokou had come and they were all standing or sitting on their bikes. It rained and there was much spitting. Small children shouted imperiously, 'Small children can't see', and all the adults shuffled obediently to one side.

On Sunday afternoon we were bussed into town to attend the closing ceremony of the Third National Games. An ancient general, one of the great military leaders of the Liberation War, Zhu De, announced 'The games are closed', and the audience opposite held up coloured cards to create giant composite pictures of healthy athletes and then turned them round to spell out 'Friendship First, Competition Second'. Thousands of athletes marched by, swinging their arms. They were arranged by province and divided by troops of gentlemen in white who goose-stepped between them. This was followed by a football match. Liaoning v. Guangdong ended in a 'Friendship First' draw. 'Competition Second' takes the edge off the attack, especially in the goal area. There was much picking up and dusting down of felled opponents and kissing of scorers who looked positively guilty.

In premature celebration of National Day, the Languages Institute threw a colourful tea party that evening. The colour was mainly provided by the food. There was bright yellow lemonade, a pink and green iced birthday cake for the nation, sweets and Peony cigarettes. All students were expected to perform. This was one thing that the British Council had not prepared us for. We should have been sent on a compulsory week to Cecil Sharp House to learn English folksongs and country dancing. The North Koreans, all dressed in national costume – crumpled blue-and-white silk dresses with great bows on the bosom for the women and amazingly ill-cut three-piece suits for the men – formed a perfect choir and sang awful North Korean songs. The

Albanians were almost as polished but eschewed national dress. The North Koreans looked as if they had been picked as a team but the Albanians were physically very varied. Some were astoundingly beautiful, especially a dark-eyed girl mysteriously called Arthur, but others were distinctly mis-shapen. The Italians sang rousing revolutionary songs, the best being Daniela's solo rendering of 'Bandiera Rossa', although she squeaked on the final high note. Unprepared and embarrassed, the only ensemble work that we British students all knew was 'Old MacDonald Had a Farm'.

After a weekend of entertainment, the serious business of learning Chinese began on Monday morning.

The First Chinese Reader

Classes were held in the teaching block of the Languages Institute, an enormous building on the far side of the campus. It took some time to get there, past the canteen, the boys' dormitory and another grey block, behind which was the Xuanquan ta, the Propaganda Pagoda or Propaganda Tower. This was a small concrete obelisk, a sort of miniature Cleopatra's Needle, painted yellow, with peeling slogans on red cartouches on all four sides. It stood in a circular flowerbed with a few drooping plum plush coxcomb flowers ('a medicinal herb') surrounded by a box hedge and it was there that we gathered to get on the bus when summoned to go on outings.

We entered the teaching building through what I subsequently discovered was the back door. Weeks later, losing my way, I found the front door and our very own twice-lifesize statue of Chairman Mao in whitewashed concrete. He was wearing a cosy concrete overcoat and had one arm raised. He appeared to be saluting himself, for on the opposite side of Xueyuan bei lu (North Institute Road) was the Institute for Petroleum Studies with its identical Mao statue. On the concrete pillars flanking the main entrance of the Languages Institute, just in front of the Chairman, the name of the institute was inscribed in Chairman Mao's own fine calligraphy. It was a black day for institutes when Chairman Hua Guofeng took over as Mao's temporary successor in April 1976 because his handwriting was ugly and jerky.

Most nationalities were taught separately. We had two language teachers. Hu Laoshi (Teacher Hu) was a tall middle-aged man with little round glasses and a voice that rose to a squeak at moments of crisis. He was somewhat dishevelled and wore ancient grey trousers which had been mended in the seat by the village tailor in Wudaokou. The tailor's favoured method of patching was to affix, not a square, but a circular patch which he carefully stitched in a series of circles, forming a tempting target pattern. Hu Laoshi was gentle and easy to tease and he seemed not to mind too much. Tian Laoshi was younger, with a sharp face and narrow eyes, and was very much in charge. It was he who handed out the textbooks, which looked dispiritingly like the *First Chinese Reader* that we all knew and loathed. He instructed us to buy three different kinds of notebook: a *bijibenr* for notes, two *zuoyebenr* for classwork and a *zuowenbenr* for essays. He was interrupted in his shopping list by Fu Laoshi, the small, pebble-glassed man who had met us at the airport and who was the cadre (or 'responsible official') for all the overseas students. We called him 'Frank' since he spoke very good English and would announce that he was going to speak 'very frankly' whenever he embarked upon one of his many chastisements. Fu Laoshi handed out to each student 25 feet's worth of *bupiao* or cotton coupons, without which we could acquire no cotton, and offered us free medical care but said we would have to pay for our own abortions.

Every morning, except Sunday, we had language lessons

from eight to twelve with a twenty-minute break in the middle. The lessons were uninspiring. The textbook was uninspired. The text consisted either of a heroic episode of recent history or a brief retelling of two 'folk' stories. These were the only ones deemed sufficiently correct to have survived the Cultural Revolution. Virtually all of China's traditional culture had been condemned as backward, superstitious or worse. The 'new' socialist person should only enjoy new socialist art-forms and new socialist stories.

It was quite difficult to tell why these two stories were viewed as correct. One was about Mr Dongguo and the wolf. Unlike Little Red Riding Hood, who had to rely upon the peasantry to save her, Mr Dongguo outwitted the wolf himself. The second story told of the blind men who tried to describe an elephant. As each one of them felt a different bit, they were unable to agree on the totality. There was no apparent political content to the story, correct or otherwise, and it was not strictly a Chinese folk tale either, for I am told it originates in the Upanishads.

Having answered questions on the text we proceeded to the exercises which related to the new vocabulary and grammatical constructions that had appeared in the text. Homework was set.

At ten o'clock every morning the entire nation, including all the students in the Languages Institute, downed tools for eight minutes. Over the tannoy, a short broadcast with nice bouncy music led the nation in a series of calisthenic exercises, toe-touching and star-jumping, the better to continue with our revolutionary tasks. There was no coffee or tea break and neither of these beverages was available either in the teaching block or in the far-off canteen, so all you could do was jump up and down or watch other students jumping up and down.

On Tuesday afternoons, lest Satan find work for idle hands, we had *laodong* or 'manual labour'. This was the most political of our activities. Following Mao's instruction that we should 'Learn from the peasants', we were supposed to make a physical contribution to the revolution and, at the same time, understand how hard the heroic peasants worked and how they did not despise any task. For Chinese students and intellectuals, the most heroic form of manual labour was shovelling manure but the Languages Institute probably thought this would have been going too far and might provoke official complaints – a pity really, because the Canadian students, who were almost all terribly serious Marxist-Leninists, would have loved to shovel dung. Most Tuesday afternoons, we were faced with a heap of rubble that had been deposited overnight on the disused tennis-court. We shovelled it somewhere else, only to find that a remarkably similar heap of rubble had returned to the tennis-court on the following Tuesday. I toyed with the idea of marking a few broken bricks to prove the point.

There were occasional variations on the heap of rubble. One Tuesday afternoon we were required to demolish a small brick shed. This proved surprisingly easy. Proper cement appeared to be rare in China and most brick structures were put together with what was, effectively, a bit of mud. You only had to push a brick and it fell off. I tried not to lean on too many walls after that. Another Tuesday afternoon, we were sent to weed the ditches around the edge of the playing-field. What we were pulling up were the few sparse clumps of grass still struggling to survive. I missed grass in China. And, as autumn turned into winter and leaves fell and were thriftily swept up, I missed greenery in general. I was outraged at the idea of eradicating grass but we were told that mosquitoes hid in it and that they constituted the sort of pests whose eradication had been personally ordered by Chairman Mao in 1958. I tried to save the grass on the grounds that mosquitoes, as far as I knew, lived in stagnant water, but this piece of bourgeois science was ignored and I was told to get back to the job.

On Wednesday afternoons we had compulsory sport, something most of us had avoided since leaving school. We ran laps of the playing-field. On very good days we were issued with bamboo swords and taught *taijijian*, a swash-

buckling version of *taijiquan* (*quan* means 'fist'; *jian* means 'sword'). We put shots. Most of the girls present refused to try, in defiance of Chairman Mao's sporting instruction, 'Develop your strength; defend the Motherland', and one Spanish girl had to be helped away when she dropped the shot on her foot, but I discovered to my alarm that I could put the shot quite a long way. We were also issued with hand-grenades and practised hand-grenade throwing. Though we all pretended to take the pins out with our teeth, these were ancient pin-less hand-grenades, shaped like little brown bottles. I sometimes wondered if the British Council knew that we were undergoing guerrilla training at the tax-payers' expense.

On Friday afternoons we had two-hour China Knowledge classes in which we would read a short article from the *People's Daily*. One such article, though it had nothing to do with China, was very good. It was on the American election system, and for the first time I actually understood what it was all about – British newspapers always seemed to assume you knew. Another was about some mysterious islands. It took a trip to the Embassy and consultation of the *Times Atlas* in the library there before I realized that these were the Paracels. Uninhabited and uninhabitable, they rise out of the South China Sea on top of oil and natural gas fields. Various nations had therefore sent boats to plant flags on them and claim them. Then there was the ill-fated Sino-Vietnamese War. This vanished from China Knowledge classes as the débâcle became increasingly apparent and rumours arose of desertion, death and ignominious return in undecorated coffins. Chinese soldiers, taught throughout the Vietnam War that the Vietnamese were their close comrades-in-arms, were said (though not by our teachers) to have been mobilized and dispatched to the front where they discovered to their horror that they were supposed to attack their erstwhile comrades.

After less than three weeks of incredibly boring classes, we were sent off for our first experience of *kaimen banxue* or 'open-door schooling'. This was a prolonged version of manual labour in which we went out every day for a week to a brigade belonging to a People's Commune, to assist the peasants with their manual labour and learn from them.

People's Communes were the agricultural unit of organization. Of considerable size, they were divided into brigades
and teams (approximating to former villages, large and
small). Peasants worked the land communally, with only tiny
patches of ground allocated for family vegetable planting. In
return for communal labour, each household received a
small annual payment in cash but was otherwise paid in
produce: oil, eggs, grain, firewood and so on.

The Sijiqing ('Green throughout the seasons') People's
Commune was only a half-hour bus ride from the Foreign
Languages Institute, just beside the New Summer Palace.
Longevity Hill and its gold-tiled temple and walkways were
clearly visible to the north, with the Western Hills behind. To
the south-east, the sixteenth-century pagoda of the Temple
of Benevolence and Longevity stood tall in the fields. As
'open-door schooling' implied not only manual labour but
also learning, we spent the mornings in the commune's
meeting-room which was lined with huge glass jars contain-
ing prize-winning red peppers and tomatoes, yellow
sweetcorn and great white turnips. Our feet froze as we listened to interminable tales of how class enemies had tried to
interfere with vegetable production (by leaving the covers off
the greenhouses in winter or making ridiculous suggestions
like growing strawberries in winter) and learnt of the steady
rise in production statistics. We also visited the school where
an essay in English was pinned on the wall in our honour: 'I
am turnip. I am big veg. It's time to let me out. Oh, here
comes Grandpa Li. "How do you, Grandpa Li?" "How do
you, big turnip?"'

On the first day we prepared spring onions for market. We
had to squat all afternoon as we tore off the papery outer
leaves and tied the spring onions into regular bundles. It was
only then that I realized why the Chinese wore very baggy

trousers with much extra cloth in the crotch area. Squatting is not too uncomfortable if you can spread your legs wide and sit well back on your haunches, but it is the shape of the trousers (or lack of it) that tells.

The next two afternoons were dismal, rainy and cold. We were set to *kun baicai* or tie up Chinese cabbage with bits of rice straw to make it heart and to keep the inner leaves as white as possible. Each of us was given a bundle of rice straw to carry on our backs as we needed both hands free. The whole process was desperately inefficient for the pieces of rice straw were very short and broke easily. Worse, a Chinese cabbage seen close to in the field is enormous and resistant to bundling. I could only just get both arms round a cabbage and had to hug it very tight and then, still hugging as best I could, get a piece of rice straw round it and tie it up. Chinese cabbage is also surprisingly hairy. All the hugging gave Rose and me an itchy red-spotted rash all the way up our arms.

Our teachers also had to participate in manual labour, and we got a lot of pleasure out of watching Hu Laoshi trying to bundle cabbages. He was absolutely useless. We stumbled along our rows, backs aching and arms itching painfully, cursing the cabbage and the lack of tensile strength in the rice straw, but we made progress. When I looked back and saw Hu Laoshi on the horizon, he was still stuck on his second cabbage. He'd stand up to ease his back and look at it. A perfectionist, he'd then bend down to adjust the rice straw which would immediately break and he'd have to start all over again. He was an object-lesson in ivory-towerism (the inability of intellectuals to handle anything practical) and the pressing need for a revolution in education, if you took agricultural prowess as the determining factor. Which they did at the time.

Fortunately for my itching arms, we soon moved on to building the winter greenhouses in which cucumbers and tomatoes were to be planted. To build the walls we piled earth into a frame of wooden planks and then pounded it down in layers. This was a building technique that had been used in China for millennia: parts of the city wall of Anyang built in the same way nearly 3,000 years ago can still be seen in Zhengzhou, the provincial capital of Henan province. The Great Wall was originally built this way. I made the mistake of telling the peasants this. They told me I was wrong: it was built of brick. I tried to tell them that it was faced with brick in the Ming dynasty but they knew it was a capitalist lie because they'd seen the Great Wall.

Once our walls were ready, sticks of bamboo were then set in them and bent over to form an arch. Plastic sheeting was stretched over the bamboo frame and, on cold nights, this was covered with very thick rolls of straw matting to keep the vegetables warm. As the sun shone almost every day throughout the winter, the greenhouses were quite efficient and could be ploughed flat in spring.

Conversation with the peasants was interesting. I was made to feel a freak for being unmarried at twenty-seven. I turned my boyfriend into a fiancé which consoled them somewhat. I thought there was an official campaign in favour of late marriage (as part of the birth-control pro-gramme) but it had obviously failed in Sijiqing People's Commune. Poor Rose, her 'fiancé' was thirty-seven. 'How can you like someone that old?' they asked. Mostly we talked prices. How much is a pair of trousers? (Mass intake of horrified breath.) How much is a television? How much is a house? (Mass scream.) I read later that the Scottish doctor who had gone out to tend to the first British diplomats to settle in Peking had had almost identical conversations with the builders working on the Embassy in 1866. They, too, wanted to know how much trousers cost.

Every day that week we had lunch in a peasant house, a simple, single-storeyed brick building set in a small courtyard with a tree and two smaller side wings. The front of the house, from the waist up, consisted almost entirely of south-facing windows with a plain wooden lattice, and there was a chimney with a cover in the form of a funny little square pavilion with a roof along whose eaves were rows of little clay doves. Chickens pecked and scratched in the courtyard and we squatted there on sunny days, eating bowls of home-made noodles in soup with matchstick slivers of cucumber and a dab of sour-plum sauce.

To repay the hospitality and critical remarks of the peasants, a performance was arranged for the last day. With much effort and despite a serious shortage of appropriate materials, I constructed paper masks so that we could enact the story of Mr Dongguo and the wolf which we felt sure they would understand, although I noticed that Tian Laoshi took the trouble to tell the assembled village the story beforehand, just in case. We rounded off our performance with the British national song, 'Old MacDonald Had a Farm'.

The Ceremony of Entering into Traffic

The Foreign Languages Institute was some miles from the centre of Peking and was itself huge; the distance from the dormitories to the teaching block alone was sufficient to require a bicycle. We discovered that a worker-peasant-soldier student of English in Canton, unaware of the sprinkling of French idioms in modern English and not helped by his dictionary which was strong on tractor parts and Stalinist slogans but ignored bourgeois affectations, had translated *rite de passage* as 'the ceremony of entering into traffic'. Though concerned about driving on the other side of the road and alarmed at the number of lumbering buses that pulled in and out of the bicycle lanes, we were nevertheless keen to enter into traffic.

Despite the fact that there seemed to be millions of bicycles on the streets, new bicycles were hard to come by. Families could take up to a year to save collectively for a bicycle and even then they could only *apply* to buy one. Supply was not guaranteed. Foreigners had to buy their bicycles in the Friendship Store near the Embassy quarter. One afternoon, soon after we arrived, we set off *en masse* with our pockets stuffed with money. The local brand of bicycle was the Flying Pigeon, huge, black, gearless and pretty well invariably a man's bike. Ladies' cycles were almost non-existent. I did not feel confident about buying one with a cross-bar and having to do that complex masculine movement of crossing my legs and swinging one gracefully over the back, particularly at moments of crisis in Peking traffic, so I bought a silly little sea-green machine (an internal import from Canton) which had tiny wheels, modelled on the Moulton. Like the Flying Pigeon it had no gears, and it was so badly engineered that I spent most of the subsequent year panting along, miles behind everyone else and expending ten times the effort.

Though we had already tried out our bicycles on the second floor of the Friendship Store, swerving around the counters, the trip back to the Languages Institute was an ordeal. We had to travel for about six miles along most of the North Circular Road. From the Embassy quarter of Jianguomen, it ran northwards into fields and then west towards the university area. We had chosen it because, unlike its namesake in London, it was, in those days, almost bare of traffic so we judged it safer than the city streets with their buses and floods of bikes. It had not, however, occurred to us to question the quality-control system in the Flying Pigeon factory. We assumed that heroic workers would produce perfect bikes under all conditions. Punctures appeared the moment we left the Friendship Store. Very early on I had to abandon my chain-guard (apparently made from the same soft metal as milk-bottle tops) and roll up one trouser leg. Pedals fell off. Handlebars twisted at the slightest movement of the wrist. We limped, some on foot, back to the Languages Institute in pitch darkness.

In the country that invented bureaucracy thousands of

years ago, you weren't allowed simply to buy a bike. It had to be registered on payment of an annual fee. A number plate was then officially fixed to the rear mudguard (if you still had one) and an on-the-spot fine of 20 yuan (a third of a month's wages) could be exacted by a traffic policeman for failure to display your licence plate. Similar fines could be demanded if you rode along carrying an open umbrella or a passenger. Jim and Gerry were caught at the bottom of the road that ran down the southern side of the university and Jim was fined because Gerry was riding on his carrier.

Getting a licence plate was as complicated as anything else in China at the time. First you needed to produce your residence permit or, in our case, official student card. This was a tiny red plastic wallet which had to carry a photograph of the bearer and multiple administrative stamps and signatures. There was no such thing as an instant photo booth in Peking so we had to make a booking at the photographer's studio in Wudaokou. The studio had a blue back-drop and you sat for what felt like hours without blinking, your head held uncomfortably in a metal frame. It then took a week for the resultant mug-shots to be developed and printed.

Once the bike was legalized and all the bits that were going to drop off had done so, bicycling became quite a pleasure. Peking lies on a flat plain, enclosed only to the fairly distant north-west by the Western Hills, and the roads in the agricultural suburbs were long and empty. From the Institute, Xueyuan lu (Institute Road) led south, almost to Deshengmen (Gate of the Victory of Virtue), one of the few bits of the city wall still standing, huge and grey with an elegant tiled roof. The road ran along a high earthen embankment which, upon investigation of a much-defaced stele at its southern end, turned out to be the remains of the city wall built by the Mongols in the mid-thirteenth century.

On the other side of the road were fields. Early in the morning, as mist rose from the ground, peasants in black padded cotton, their trousers tied at the ankles with black bindings, bent over the fine green shoots of winter wheat or weeded between rows of cabbages. From Deshengmen, a diagonal road, the only one in the chessboard city, led past the red walls and golden roofs of the palace of Prince Chun, grandfather of the last Emperor of China, Henry Aisin-gioro Puyi. It had previously been inhabited by another

imperial family member, Yihui, well-known as a poet who celebrated the lilacs that grew beside the palace pond. In 1975, it was said that the Panchen Lama lived there.

Apart from the red walls of the palace, the diagonal road leading towards the Drum and Bell Towers was lined, like most of Peking's streets, with low, grey-roofed shops. They had delicate lattice windows of dark wood pasted with white paper which showed off the lattice patterns to fine effect. My favourite design was composed of irregularly placed triangles, the 'cracked ice' pattern. Along the eaves were delicately carved boards, some with cloud patterns, some with birds amongst branches of plum blossom, some with brocade patterns scattered with lotus flowers. Almost all of these shops, which faced on to the street, had been turned into houses, and the strip of ground in front of them into front gardens with washing-lines and sunflowers in summer and oleanders potted in oil drums.

Within the city, the volume of traffic increased. Rivers of cyclists flowed around buses and lorries, all ringing their repeater bells constantly. No one ever pointed out that the constant ringing of thousands of bicycle bells lessened their warning effect, and as buses and lorries treated their horns in the same way, the streets were a cacophony. At major cross-roads, traffic police occupied traffic islands. Some stood on large concrete barrels, whistles hanging from their lower lips ready to burst the eardrums of traffic violators, their arms constantly circling in incomprehensible balletic movement. Others had little towers to live in, equipped with tannoys so that they could single out miscreants and address them publicly, with amplification. The inhabitants of the towers operated the traffic lights manually and often with apparent malice. The traffic lights themselves were baffling. There was red which meant stop, green which meant go, and green and amber together which meant that you could turn right but not left. Since the Chinese drive on the right-hand side of the road, it was only a left turn that took you dangerously across traffic. As I stood for the first time in a crowd of cyclists at Xinjiekou (New Crossroads), wondering what green and yellow meant, a voice blared through the tannoy, 'Foreign friend, you may now turn right.' All the other cyclists stopped and stared, fascinated, as I, blushing, made my manoeuvre.

Wherever you went, you had to park your bicycle in an official bicycle park for the sum of 2 fen. The fierce old lady in charge took the money and handed out two little slips of bamboo, one with a loop of string threaded through a hole in one end. They both bore the same number. You looped the string over the handlebars, locked your bike (very important) and took the other little tally with you. On your return, you showed the tally to the lady and collected your bike. This was often a hugely difficult task. All bicycles in Peking (with the exception of my horrid sea-green one) were black and looked exactly the same. Even finding mine could be difficult as the parking attendant would often tidy up her bike park, moving hundreds of vehicles in an attempt to keep it looking nice.

Cycling in the evening was interesting. There were no bicycle lights at all. On the second evening in Peking, as we were taken home from an Embassy dinner in the Embassy minibus, I remarked upon this to the driver who was negotiating his way through pitch-dark streets. Figures swerved suddenly into the headlights and he muttered, as he peered grimly into the night, that there had been bicycle lights before the Cultural Revolution. His tone carried the dangerous implication that the Cultural Revolution was not altogether a good thing.

There weren't any traffic lights after nine o'clock in the evening either, because their human controllers went home, and though there was less traffic at night, its invisibility and unpredictability in these uncontrolled circumstances was frightening.

As the rivers of cyclists flowed interminably, it seemed as if nothing would stop them. They were disinclined to take notice of traffic policemen shouting at them and they ignored any amount of furious whistling. There was, however, one thing that did bring the traffic to an undisciplined halt and that was the sight of the British military attaché performing the ceremony of entering into traffic as he cycled to the office. Wearing a tweed suit, his briefcase dangling from his handlebars, Colonel Greenwood demonstrated mastery of the Highway Code. He looked both ways before leaving the diplomatic compound and his hand-signals were a delight. He flapped one arm vigorously when he was about to slow down. He even did that complicated circling motion of the arm indicating that he was about to turn left. Wise Chinese cyclists parked their bikes at the kerb and leaned on their handlebars to watch this elegant performance; the unwise cycled on with their heads twisted round to catch a last glimpse and rode into each other. The crashing of bikes all around him had absolutely no effect on Colonel Greenwood as he made his stately way to the Embassy. And since he always went home for lunch, there were four performances a day.

Kiessling's Canteen

Though Fu Laoshi had issued us with 25 feet's worth of cotton coupons, an extra concession was made as winter approached. None of us was really prepared for the average winter temperature of minus 5 degrees Centigrade or even colder temperatures on the occasional overcast days. We were summoned to the Institute shop which we rarely visited as it stocked even less than the general store in Wudaokou. An enormous mountain of blue cotton-padded winter coats was piled in a corner and we were invited to purchase them without having to use nearly half our precious coupons. The winter coat came in two styles – single- or double-breasted, each with a brown fake fur collar – and was unbelievably heavy. I chose the less dashing single-breasted type, but only because it weighed slightly less.

All Chinese citizens were issued with coupons for grain, oil, eggs and cotton (and other commodities at times of short supply). You were only allowed to buy these things if you handed over the appropriate number of coupons, and you could get change in coupons of smaller denominations if required. (Foreign students were not issued with grain coupons because we were not capable of eating enough rice to make a dent in the national economy.) Coupons were only locally exchangeable. If you were going on a long trip which would involve eating or buying, you had to apply for special nationally valid coupons or else carry all your rice with you which helped to fill up railway carriages to an uncomfortable degree. Train travellers did seem to take huge sacks of rice with them but they could only stay away until they'd eaten their luggage. It was like rationing in the War when people complained if weekend visitors didn't bring their own allowances of butter and sugar.

We were only indirectly affected by grain rationing. When we went to the local restaurant in Wudaokou, we often ate big steamed bread rolls called *mantou*. Although they tasted a bit like warm laundry, they were useful for mopping up gravy and filling in corners. At the beginning of the month they were made of white flour. By the end of the month, when supplies of white flour were exhausted, they were made of brown flour. Brown flour was despised and brown rice did not exist. Whiteness was all. Our enthusiasm for brown buns was thought most peculiar.

The Languages Institute's efforts to entertain us contin-ued throughout the autumn. On 1 October, National Day, we were bussed off to two parks. The first was the Sun Yat-sen Memorial Park, just to the west of the Forbidden City, the site of the Ming dynasty altar to the earth and harvests. Inside the entrance was a white marble *pailou*, a ceremonial archway, topped with blue-glazed roof tiles. This was the Kettler Memorial, erected in memory of the German Minister, Baron Clement August von Kettler, who had been assassinated on 20 June 1900 as he made his way to the old Chinese foreign ministry (the Zongli yamen) in the north-east of the city, to protest about the Boxer threat to

Peking's foreign legations. The memorial arch used to stand on the spot where he fell, in Chongwenmen dajie (known as Hatamen Street by foreign residents), but was moved to the park in 1918.

The white marble altar, a huge square terrace (for in traditional Chinese cosmography the earth is square), stood to the right, approached by a path bordered by massive cypress trees, reputed to be nearly a thousand years old. Standing amongst the trees, Chinese families who had been issued with entrance tickets to the park watched exhibition games of Chinese chess (*weiqi*). Special boards set up against the grey tree-trunks showed how the games were going. They had bought loaves of sweet bread to chew and inflatable plastic spotted deer for their children to play with. The Song and Dance Ensemble of the People's Liberation Army sang over-amplified songs and there was a conjuring show. The conjuror pretended to roast a live duck in a microwave oven. Though he produced a cardboard roast duck, the original live white one never reappeared. He would have been hounded out of children's parties in London. He was also good at producing gasping live goldfish from nowhere.

Next we moved on to the Yiheyuan, the New Summer Palace, not far from the Languages Institute and visible across the fields when we laboured at open-door schooling. There had been summer palaces on the site since 1153, taking advantage of the hill and lake nearby. The lake had been enlarged over the centuries, the most notable improvements being made by the Qianlong Emperor in the eighteenth century for his mother's sixtieth birthday. He named the hill 'Longevity Hill' in her honour and had several separate garden areas constructed on the site, many copied from famous gardens in southern China. A massive temple was built against Longevity Hill, with green- and yellow-tiled pavilions; and a covered walkway with vermilion columns and brightly painted ceilings ran along the side of the lake.

Similar performances, plastic deer and sweet bread were available in the park, and here we saw our first celebrity. Chen Yonggui had been the leader of the Dazhai production brigade, the most revolutionary agricultural brigade in China where agricultural collectivization and the communal life had been carried much further than anywhere else. The Dazhai peasants gave up their private plots of land, lived in dormitory blocks and ate in communal kitchens, and their production figures were supposed to have soared as a result of all that communal revolutionary fervour. As a reward, Chen Yonggui was brought to Peking to be part of the government. He had a dark brown, incredibly wrinkled face, a hand-rolled cigarette permanently on the go and, even in Peking, always wore a white towel on his head, to keep the honest sweat from rolling down his brow, though the wrinkles would probably have dispersed it sideways.

In late October, it was customary for all the inhabitants of Peking to rush off to the Western Hills, north of the New Summer Palace, to admire the colours of the autumn leaves. We joined the mass exodus. The entire population of Peking was struggling up the mountains. 'What's behind this hill?' 'More hills.' A tannoy set up on a porcelain pagoda broadcast messages: 'Mountain climbers, take care. Do not destroy monuments. Do not destroy trees and flowers. Will the party from the No. 7 East is Red Primary School go to the west gate straight away?'

That month there was also an international football match. An ostensibly friendly team from New Zealand was to play the Chinese national team, drawn mostly from the People's Liberation Army and called the 1 August team after

Army Day. It was a much faster game than the usual 'Friendship First, Competition Second' matches. A Chinese striker scored beautifully but then, when the Chinese goalkeeper was awarded a penalty kick and the entire New Zealand team lined up right in front of him, making the manoeuvre extremely difficult to execute, the crowd became restive. This tactic (apparently sanctioned by the international football authorities) was new to them. They howled and booed. The 'new rule' was explained over the tannoy, with an appeal to keep calm, which was largely ignored. Such was the ugly mood of the crowd that the New Zealand students among us feared repercussions. Apparently the New Zealand Youth Orchestra had achieved great things for New Zealand-China understanding and the football team seemed set on undoing it all.

On another afternoon we were taken to visit a mysterious institution called the Peking Trusting Company where we had an equally mysterious lecture on Zhang Guotao. One of the founding members of the Chinese Communist Party, he had studied in Russia and had even interpreted for Lenin at a meeting with Chinese railway workers. He attended the Congress of the Toilers of the East in 1922 but quarrelled with Mao very early on and eventually retired to Hong Kong to write his memoirs. Described in a biographical dictionary as 'regularly excoriated in orthodox Maoist histories', Zhang was associated with the (evil) 'Twenty-eight Bolsheviks' who had studied at Sun Yat-sen University in Moscow and, in Mao's eyes, had become excessively pro-Soviet. Though not really part of that group, Zhang was added on as a minor accomplice, making the total 'Twenty-eight and a Half Bolsheviks'. Mao's suppression of the 'Twenty-eight Bolsheviks' in 1930–1 was officially described as the third of the Ten Great Struggles, in this case against the 'third left opportunist line'. The conclusion of the lecture was that Zhang Guotao, despite association with the third left opportunist line, was in fact a right-flightest and splittist. Right-flightism and Splittism must be opposed.

The same evening we saw another film. *The Path-breakers* was about the painful establishment of the Daqing oilfield in northern China in 1959. Daqing eventually became the industrial equivalent of Chen Yonggui's Dazhai brigade, a revolutionary path-breaker. I can't remember much about the film as I found it unaccountably difficult to stay awake. Whenever I woke up, it seemed that no progress had been made. The highpoint in the creation of Daqing apparently occurred when class enemies sabotaged the cement-mixer and Iron Man Wang leapt in and 'stirred the concrete with his body'. You could even buy a set of postcards about Daqing with a picture of Iron Man Wang flailing about in the concrete.

When the Institute wasn't busy entertaining us, we tried to entertain ourselves. The English class decided to go on a mass day-trip to Tianjin. Only a couple of hours away from Peking by train, Tianjin had been one of the treaty ports, foreign settlements set up on Chinese soil after the Opium Wars in the nineteenth century, and was rumoured still to be full of Western architecture and Western-style restaurants where you could drink coffee and eat ice-cream. Preparations for the two-hour train-ride took considerable organization. Each student card had to be gathered up and permission for the expedition sought from Fu Laoshi. Then, armed with an official letter from the Institute, we had to go to the Public Security Bureau in Nanchizi, a little street which ran down the east side of the Forbidden City. There we each acquired a travel permit. At that time, foreigners were not allowed to travel about China without one. When we arrived at Peking railway station on the day of departure, the first thing we had to do was find the Railway Public Security Bureau and present the travel permits for stamping.

The railway station had been built in 1958 as one of the Ten Great Buildings that marked the Great Leap Forward. It had a huge portrait of Chairman Mao over the door and little yellow-tiled pavilions perched on the roof. Every Friday evening as we went to the Embassy in the minibus, Gerry

would ask me which temple it was, with its little yellow-tiled pavilions. Every Friday I would tell him it was Peking railway station.

Train travel in China was wonderful. Even on the two-hour journey to Tianjin in the hard-seat class we sat in relative comfort. There were more expensive seats in 'soft' class, where you could get a small compartment with lace curtains and porcelain cups and a thermos for tea. Terms

like 'First Class', which smacked of privilege, had been
abolished in favour of non-judgemental descriptions of a
whole series of different types of carriage: hard seat, hard
sleeper with three rows of wooden bunks in an enormous
open carriage, soft seat, and soft sleeper with four bunks to
a compartment, each provided with blankets, pillows and
sheets. In theory, anyone could have access to any of these
but because they varied in price, and because you needed
special nationally valid oil and grain coupons if you were
going to eat away from home, only Party officials or army
officers on 'official business' ever occupied the 'soft' classes.

Outside the windows the flat North China plain passed
by. Little low grey village houses clustered together under
tall, thin catalpa trees, while the roads were lined with
poplars. These were like lollipops, for they retained only a
tiny tuft of leaves and branches at the very top which
passing mules or peasants in search of firewood could not
reach.

Upon arrival at Tianjin railway station – not as impressive
as Peking's – our first task was to find the Public Security
Bureau and have our travel permits stamped again. The
railway waiting-room was distracting. Its walls were lined
with posters. As political campaign succeeded political campaign (all under the overall banner of the Cultural
Revolution), public places were festooned with artwork. In
Tianjin, two major themes were evident. There were hand-
painted posters attacking the fourteenth-century novel *Shui
hu zhuan* (*The Water Margin*), which none of us had read, and
Lin Biao, Mao's erstwhile close comrade-in-arms and head
of the Party's Military Affairs Committee but currently not
only dead but also disgraced and mysteriously associated
with Confucius, another disgraced figure with whom he
could not possibly have had anything to do as Confucius had

been dead for some 1,300 years. *The Water Margin* posters singled out the novel's main character, Song Jiang, and accused him of capitulationism. This was baffling since none of us could understand how a single episode in an ancient novel could be associated with the current campaign to increase northern grain yields until they overtook those of the much more productive south. The message on the posters was 'Defeat Song Jiang's capitulationism and leap over the Yangtze'.

Extensive study of *The Water Margin* after our visit did little to clarify the matter. Song Jiang was a good official, unusually fair and helpful and loved by all. He became a bandit after murdering his wife, who had been extremely unfaithful, and for about a thousand chapters he led the life of a bandit, but still rather a good and helpful one. The only possible flaw in his character in Cultural Revolution terms was his continuing loyalty to the Emperor which could be interpreted as a capitulationist stance, I suppose.

The posters of Lin Biao showed him lying, ill-shaven, on a bed with his shoes on (an unthinkably decadent pose – whoever kept their shoes on in such a position?). A bubble coming out of his head read, 'Thinks: Must restore the Old Order' (that is, Confucianism). Other posters showed him, less comfortably, boiling like a missionary in a cauldron labelled 'Extreme Confucianism'.

As there were fewer foreigners in Tianjin than in Peking, we were not only stared at and remarked upon but also found ourselves the centre of a huge crowd. I didn't mind too much and was prepared to perform, singing the current kindergarten hit, 'I love Peking's Tiananmen', to an apprecia- tive crowd at a bus stop. Gerry found it all rather difficult. He went into a public gents but was utterly unable to perform in front of two hundred pairs of interested eyes and nearly died before we reached the main object of our trip to Tianjin – Kiessling's, where the riff-raff were excluded from the lavatories.

The Café Kiessling, originally Kiessling and Bader's, had been the best tea-room and restaurant in Tianjin throughout its treaty-port heyday. In fact it was so essential to the well-being of the city's foreign inhabitants that it opened a branch in the beach resort of Beidaihe during the summer so that they wouldn't starve. The original building was situated on a roundabout in the centre of Tianjin. It had, rather unimaginatively, been renamed the Tianjin Canteen but in the downstairs area it still sold coffee beans, and Smarties in flimsy cardboard tubes with little plastic caps. Upstairs was a wonderful Thirties dining-room with bevelled mirrors, heavy brown curved furniture and a gallery stuffed with Chinese families tucking in to knickerbocker glories and chicken Stroganoff. The waiters were as much original fittings as the furniture and spoke a comfortable Chinglish – '*Nin yao bu yao chi borscht ma?*' ('Would you like borscht?'), '*Jige ice-cream?*' ('How many ice-creams?'), '*Yao bu yao chocolate sauce?*' ('With or without chocolate sauce?'). We ate bread and butter, borscht, delicious and with cream, chicken Stroganoff with champignons de Paris, and beef stew sizzling in individual cauldrons; then ice-cream (with chocolate sauce), *petits fours* and coffee in glasses, Russian-style. All this was accompanied by gin, bottled at the Tianjin Winery. The whole vast meal cost 6 yuan each (then about £1.50). On the way out we bought bags of coffee beans which were utterly unobtainable in Peking.

Wandering through the streets after a very filling lunch, we came across our first government pawn-shop. I later found that there were similar shops in Peking but this first discovery was a revelation. Members of the public could bring in 'antiques' and sell them to the state. If they were not of museum standard, they were offered for re-sale to passing foreigners of whom there weren't many in Tianjin at the time. I bought several embroidered pillow ends – square silk embroideries that fitted on long silk pillows used on the raised brick beds (*kang*) which had once been fixtures in northern homes. I also acquired a strange padded silk oblong in aquamarine and orange with much embroidery – a Manchu skirt, I was later told.

When it was time to return to Peking and escape from the interested crowds, our first duty was, once again, to visit the Tianjin railway station Public Security Bureau to have our travel permits stamped and to offer the good news that traffic in Tianjin could now flow freely as we were leaving. When we got back to Peking railway station, we had to revisit the Public Security Bureau there to have our travel permits stamped as evidence of our return before the hour-long journey to the Languages Institute in the outer suburbs.

The supplies of coffee beans from Kiessling's lasted for months. Every Sunday we had a communal breakfast which involved much planning. On the previous Friday evening we would stop at the Friendship Store for tiny little medicinal bottles of milk, small brown loaves, butter, pâté and caviare which we would then store on Sarah's north-facing window-sill. On Sunday morning the coffee beans were ground slowly in a tiny hand-mill, mixed with hot water from a thermos flask and served in a small porcelain teapot in the shape of a cat with one raised paw (the spout). Perfectionists might complain that the coffee was tepid and the butter often rancid but we felt that Sunday breakfast was a luxury achieved in the face of considerable odds.

Letters of Determination

Almost as soon as we arrived in China, we were informed that yet another campaign was in the offing. It seemed that the minute the impetus of one campaign slowed, another must be introduced, to maintain political fervour. In November, the Revolution in Education officially began. The Minister of Education was apparently guilty of ivory-towerism, supporting 'big-name' universities and failing to understand the greater potential of learning from the peasants. He was characterized as a Chinese Mr Gradgrind, preferring the equivalent of Linnaean classification and Latin tags to the simple peasant view of a horse as a beast of burden made to be whipped and starved to the point of collapse.

Wires were strung across the canteen dining-room just above head height. Poster-sized sheets of deep pink, sea-green and pale yellow paper were stuck to them, like brilliantly coloured tea-towels. Essays were written on the papers criticizing the Rightist Revisionist Wind on the Educational Front, mixed metaphors not apparently being frowned upon. One way to demonstrate your enthusiasm for the revolution was to copy down the contents of these 'big-character posters', standing in the dining-room for hours filling exercise books with endless versions of the same thing.

Our Friendship Class was stirred. Not only did they earnestly fill their notebooks with copies of the big-character posters but they also wrote Letters of Determination (*juexin xin*). Letters of Determination were written in waves, their content dictated by the current movement. In November 1975, the need to vanquish ivory-towerism and combat the Rightist Revisionist Wind on the Educational Front was combined with a call for volunteers to go and serve their country by working in Tibet. The middle-aged men and women in our Friendship Class had already upset their routines by obeying the call to come and learn English at the Foreign Languages Institute. This was supposed to help them in propaganda work among their colleagues (none of whom knew any English). Since they all had families and children in Peking and its environs, none of them wanted to go to Tibet and none of them ever imagined that they would be chosen to do so. Writing Letters of Determination about their desire to further the revolution in Tibet was a rhetorical exercise of the sort they had been through before. Their putative destination was probably the worst they could imagine. They knew that Tibet was terribly far away; that the altitude made you ill; that the Tibetans existed on an unthinkable diet of barley and rancid butter; and that they were unquestionably savages.

There was one man in our Friendship Class who was more interesting than the rest. Old Zhao was a curator at the Peking Man Museum out on the outskirts of the city at Zhoukoudian, beside the cave in which the remains of the eponymous man had been found. The first skull of

Sinanthropus pekinensis (*c.* 500,000 BC) had been excavated by the French Jesuit archaeologist Teilhard de Chardin in 1929. That this significant contribution to Chinese archaeology had been made by a foreigner was a great embarrassment, although the subsequent disappearance of the original skull during the Japanese occupation (1937–45), when it was possibly stolen by the Japanese or, even more heinous, by the Americans, was some consolation, for it demonstrated the general treachery of interfering foreigners. Face was restored when Chinese archaeologists found a lower jawbone in 1958, during the Great Leap Forward. A scholarly archaeologist, Old Zhao was clearly distressed by the political contortions that he was forced to undergo when dismissing the contribution of Teilhard de Chardin and attempting to fit the rather simple lifestyle of Peking Man into Friedrich Engels' matriarchal stage of primitive society. He was also quite unprepared for the announcement that his Letter of Determination was so convincing that he had been awarded the chance to make his contribution to society in Tibet.

A terrific send-off was arranged. Old Zhao had a huge red paper flower pinned to his chest. This was a badge of revolutionary triumph, to be worn proudly on significant occasions. Outside the canteen we lined up with our Friendship Class and hundreds of other students, all clapping wildly and feigning regret that we had not been honoured. Old Zhao climbed miserably into the back of an army lorry, weighed down by the huge bedding roll (made up of a cotton wadded mattress and thick cotton-stuffed quilt) strapped to his back. We did not see him again, though we heard much later that he had been invalided out after six months and had returned safely to his hominids.

Another sort of send-off had been planned for Gerry, one of the most linguistically gifted of our class. He had gone to university in his home town and was thoroughly homesick at the Institute. It was clear that his mother missed him dreadfully for she demonstrated her love, combined with a distinct lack of trust in the international postal service, by dispatching his Christmas parcel of Mars bars, fruit cake and tubes of Smarties as soon as he left England. It arrived in mid-October.

Before we had begun to understand the complex system of arrangements for foreign students in China, some of us

had started pressing to move on from the Institute to proper universities. The Institute was designed for beginners and, though the classes were unbelievably boring, the students who made most progress there were those who had little Chinese when they arrived. Gerry spoke wonderful Chinese and could only amuse himself in class by teasing the teachers. Many of the exercises in our textbooks concerned the exploits of various Chinese revolutionary heroes, most of whom had made the ultimate sacrifice in order to stop a runaway train or an out-of-control lorry filled with cabbages belonging to the masses. Throwing yourself in front of a lorry seemed to me an unlikely way of bringing it to a vegetable-friendly halt but we were not encouraged to question the physics of the act, only to admire the spirit of self-sacrifice. A sturdy peasant girl called Liu Hulan was threshed (literally) to death by the Japanese army of occupation because of her stoical refusal to collaborate. Dong Cunrui had been unable to find a way to attach his explosives to a bridge which he needed to blow up to stop the invading Japanese so he stood under the bridge, holding the explosives close to the structure, with the inevitable result that he figured prominently in *Elementary Chinese Book 2* and on little boys' vests.

The most mysterious of these heroes was Lei Feng who didn't do anything heroic. This became his claim to fame. He was a simple soldier in the People's Liberation Army who spent his life being helpful. He was said to have washed all his fellow-soldiers' clothing whilst they were asleep, just to be helpful. After his non-heroic death, his diary was published. In it each little act of kindness was recorded, as was his apparent desire to be a 'little rustless screw' in the giant machine of China.

I would like to be a tiny screw
So that they can put me where they want and
    screw me tight,
Whether on the arm of a powerful crane
Or in the simplest wheel.

Put me in place and screw me tight.
There I shall stay firmly put, my heart at rest.

Perhaps people will not know that I exist,
But I know that vibrating in the heart of
   a great machine
Is the life of a tiny screw.

Although I cannot be a machine all alone,
Although I can do nothing all alone,
I can serve my country and the people even so.
I know that if I stay in the background, I shall soon
Be nothing but a piece of rusty metal.

I would like to be a tiny screw
So that they can put me where they want and
   screw me tight.
I shall be happy, and in the choir of heroes
I shall tremble to hear my own passionate voice.

His entry for 15 February 1961, written in an ugly, forward-sloping hand, was typical: 'Today I took advantage of the Spring Festival holiday to cart several hundred catties* of dung to the People's Commune, to support agriculture. I gave the several hundred catties of dung to the peasants as a Spring Festival gift, to show them what was in my heart.' The phrase 'He's full of sh*t' did spring to mind.

Elementary Chinese Book 2 contained many stories about Lei Feng which were used for sentence practice. To master the necessary pronunciation for 'cross the road' we were told that 'Lei Feng helped the old lady to cross the road.' Gerry spent much time producing perfectly grammatical sentences, enunciated with all the correct tones, which suggested that Lei Feng hadn't helped the old lady to cross the road or that

* A catty in post-1949 China was equivalent to half a kilo.

the old lady hadn't wanted to cross the road but Lei Feng had made her do so. Our teachers never knew how to respond. There was usually a long silence, followed by a 'No-o-o.' 'What's wrong with the sentence?' A further long silence would follow before the teacher fell back on 'We just don't say that.'

Lei Feng's story fascinated us. He was born, so they said, in 1940 into a poor peasant family that rented land from a wicked landlord in Hunan province. His father was beaten to death by the Japanese, his elder brother, already suffering from TB, fell into the machinery in the pre-Liberation factory in which he worked as a slave. This may have given his younger brother the rustless screw idea. After her husband's death, Lei Feng's mother hanged herself from a roof-beam, a traditional method of female suicide in China. In his short life, Lei Feng managed to be a worker and a peasant and a soldier, personifying the educational experience we were supposed to emulate by studying or learning from all three. His first essay, 'I learnt to drive a tractor', was published when he was a peasant. A subsequent piece, 'I learnt to drive a bulldozer', appeared when he was a worker in the Anshan Iron and Steel Company. Though there are 306 pages devoted to him in the *Lei Feng Cidian* (*Lei Feng Dictionary*, published in 1992), all that is recorded of his death is 'On 15 August 1962, Lei Feng died at his post.' The two characters used indicated that he died either 'on duty' or 'for reasons of state'. Thoroughly irritated by the stories of his small helpfulnesses, we pressed for more information. 'Was he assassinated by class enemies?' 'We do not know.' 'Was it a cabbage lorry?' 'We do not know.' Gerry's theory, beautifully enunciated as ever, was that his fellow-soldiers, enraged by waking every day and being forced to put on clean but wet underwear, had murdered him.

Gerry had applied to study Chinese linguistics before he learnt that linguistics was only available to foreign students at Nankai University in Tianjin. Though the prospect of regular meals at Kiessling's appealed, he could not face leaving us and the relative comforts of Peking. No more Friday night minibus thoughtfully provided by the British Embassy so that we could drink in The Bell and make toasted cheese sandwiches in the electric sandwich grill. No more silly evenings crammed into Jim's room listening to *Monty Python* tapes. No more moral support from the British students. We didn't want to lose him either because we were very fond of him and he was funny. It was he who had to stop the minibus on the way back to the Institute one Friday night, asking the driver to find a '*hei difang*' (literally, a black place) because he was too full of beer to wait. Most of Peking was pretty black at night but the driver stopped immediately he was asked, embarrassingly close to several bus-stops and one of the very few street lights still on. Gerry managed to find a *hei difang* behind a heap of coal on the pavement but he fell over it and returned to the bus covered in black dust and moaning that he'd broken his ankle.

Every Friday at about midday, a white minibus would arrive outside Gerry's dormitory block to take him to Tianjin. Our cadre, Fu Laoshi, would peer about through his bottle-bottom glasses enquiring as to Gerry's whereabouts, but he never found him. Fortunately for Gerry's peace of mind, the minibus always arrived promptly on a Friday and left empty. Oddly, Fu Laoshi never mentioned Gerry's continuing presence and regular class attendance on the other six days of the week.

As it appeared that my Chinese, though not up to his, was probably good enough to get me on a university course, I opted to study Chinese history. It was the only subject that

interested me out of those on offer. Philosophy did
not mean Confucianism or Taoism but more Marxism-
Leninism-Mao Zedong Thought. Literature was strictly
confined to the very small handful of acceptable contemporary novelists who were by no means acceptable to me, and
anyway it was only offered in Shanghai. I wanted to stay in
Peking and I knew that a history course was available at
Peking University. On top of that, Peking University was a
prestigious destination, even if it was at the lowest ebb in its
history, with all the best professors still planting vegetables
in distant communes. It was the focus of political activity
and, whilst I did not harbour illusions about becoming part
of the political process, we would be allowed to read the big-
character posters put up on its campus by the students
before anyone else outside the university.

Freezing Sheets

Every female foreign student faced with a year in Peking was naturally concerned with sanitary protection. Every single one of us flew out with a suitcase stuffed with a cautious overestimate of the necessary supplies. There was nothing available in China then, not even sanitary towels. Chinese ladies made their own primitive arrangements with lavatory paper, cotton rags, even newspaper. As it turned out, we needn't have worried: with the exception of those optimists who continued to take the Pill, all periods stopped within about a month of our arrival. I was concerned and wrote to my mother for a long-distance consultation. She wrote back to say that she had spoken to a gynaecologist and the response, combined with her own experience of leaving home in the War to live in a Nissen hut at Bletchley Park (where the same thing had happened owing to a dramatic 'change of lifestyle'), was reassuring. I added my eleven-month supply of sanitary equipment to the rising Tampax mountain.

The issue of a single sheet and a single pillow-case also presented a quandary. There was a laundry in the Institute, but it offered only a weekly service. Was one prepared to sleep on the bare pillow and mattress for a whole week before one's laundry was returned? In the early days, this was not a huge problem. The sun was warm, and a quick wash and a brief session on the washing-line outside were enough to refresh the bed. I had a narrow escape at the washing-line one late October day when a rather dozy hornet attacked me. As I unpegged my sheet, I heard a sudden buzzing and swivelled my eyes to see a yellow-and-black-striped insect about two inches long, entangled in my hair. Taught as a child to stay still when attacked by wasps or bees, I froze. I seemed to be there for hours, bent slightly to one side, before the gigantic insect decided to go elsewhere. No one noticed me apparently paralysed in a strange twisted position which was probably just as well. A crowd of well-meaning and excitable Cambodian students would have made the situation much worse had they tried to rescue me. Still, it was a horrible and alien moment in a country where insects appeared so much larger and more dangerous than at home.

There were, however, some rather less alarming insects that lived in the bricks and mud of the Institute. The south-facing wall, just beside the washing-line, was a nice warm spot. Lots of students would sit and read there, leaning against the wall of the dormitory in the autumn sun. Every so often, the drowsy silence would be broken by screams as a stink-bug, toppling down from a brick bolt-hole high above, unleashed its only weapon on the sunbathers below. The stink-bugs were little greenish-brown, diamond-shaped insects with quite long legs and, when alarmed, they released a disgusting smell. They looked somehow prehistoric, like tiny dinosaurs.

As the weather grew colder, washing became more difficult. You could watch a careful housewife throw dirty water out on to the pavement and see it freeze instantly as it hit the ground. At the same time, Peking became insufferably dry, with no rain or snow and all moisture frozen in the ground. Paddy, a moth-eaten labrador passed from one British diplomatic family to another to avoid either the quarantine laws or the chore of looking after him in his degenerative old age, became electric. Giving him an affectionate pat was like being struck by lightning.

One winter afternoon I thought I'd wash my sheet myself as usual, using cold water and White Cat detergent powder (stunningly unkind to hands). I took the still dripping sheet outside to the washing-line. Within minutes, it had frozen into an enormous and very solid block, far bigger than the door. I had visions of trying to fold it smaller and ending up with lots of broken bits and having to explain this appalling treatment of Institute property to Fu Laoshi who had signed it over to me. I did eventually manage to fold it over sufficiently to get it back in through the door in one piece but it took several days to unfreeze in the dank washroom and several more days to dry.

Gracious living clearly required expenditure, and cotton coupons. I lashed out on six feet's worth of coupons for an extra sheet and a similar amount for curtaining. Unless I was prepared to sink to the more expensive polyester, I now had only twelve feet's worth left for the year and I had already promised my brother that I would supply cotton T-shirts with printed slogans from the limited range offered by the local laundry.

In theory, you could have had any characters you wanted printed on T-shirts, mackintoshes or tea-towels, but in practice, politics were, as ever, in command. An immensely tall and lanky Swedish student with a great clump of fair hair got tired of walking along city streets and having the entire population call out '*Waiguo ren*' ('Foreigner'), as if he didn't know.

Eventually he decided to ask the laundry in Wudaokou to print '*Waiguo ren*' on a T-shirt for him. The laundryman refused. He couldn't say why he wouldn't do it but he somehow knew it was wrong. If he knew it was wrong, why did everyone else say it? The same thing happened to the rest of us, all the time, although we weren't quite so visible from a distance. Wherever we went, whatever we did, there was always the insistent whisper, '*Waiguo ren*'. If you just slipped out of the Institute gates to post a letter, people staggered back, arms flailing, or flattened themselves against walls and stared. I remember one little old lady in her thick black cotton padded suit, hobbling along on bound feet, who had to clutch at a tree when I passed as she muttered '*Waiguo ren*' to herself. Since the laundry was clearly uncooperative, in the end I had to settle for 'Serve the People' on my brother's T-shirts.

One of the few people with whom we could discuss such matters was Lu Mei, a student from our Friendship Class. The daughter of an incredibly famous Chinese painter, by his second wife, she was in her late twenties. As far as I was concerned, she seemed very attractive, being not bad-looking and gifted at languages. In fact, she was something of an embarrassment to the Friendship Class because she was so much better than the others. Mei was also a snob. Born into the intellectual aristocracy, her intelligence, her familiarity with the top leaders (Zhou Enlai had attended her father's funeral) and her sophistication made her impatient with her rather ordinary fellow-students and she spent much more time with us.

Communication with Lu Mei was a great deal easier than with the average member of our Friendship Class, but even so there was a sense of things held back. Under different circumstances, if she had not been obliged to present herself as a worker-peasant-soldier student, and if we had not been obliged to assume that that was what she was, we could have communicated quite freely. She confided that an introduction to a prospective husband had been made for her. As she was nearly my age and still unmarried, such an event was pretty important. She was to dine with an army officer of some rank in Wudaokou and she had to present herself as interested but not desperate. Whether she pitched it wrongly or he just didn't like her, nothing came of this particular encounter. Poor Lu Mei – under any other regime, she would have been an acceptable, if argumentative aristocrat and her antecedents would have counted for something. Instead, with a famous cultural figure for a father and still unmarried, she was at the bottom of the revolutionary pile.

Her English was extraordinarily good. We used to pass her ancient copies of Sunday papers that came our way through the Embassy and she read them all. She got very worried about an article on hair-dye causing cancer, as she said her mother had been dyeing her hair black for decades. I'd always assumed that the Chinese, as a race, had black hair from birth to death but her confidences revealed the fact that most middle-aged Chinese dyed their hair, a surprising revelation in the face of the Cultural Revolution's ban on attention to personal appearance.

Disregarding the ban, I had my hair cut in the Languages Institute, which was in itself a sort of revelation. It cost 15p, including washing and blow-drying. The hairdresser was a frustrated Mr Teazie-Weazie, utterly fed up with the regulation pudding-basins he was required to produce. The Chinese didn't dare appear on the streets with a perm as they'd be accused (on the authority of the *People's Daily*) of being cow-ghosts and snake-spirits, so all he could do was cut, and cut straight. He begged me to allow him to perm my hair 'because Western hair is so soft', but one glance at his electrical torture corner with its strange black snake-like tubes and giant bulldog clips was enough to put me off the idea. He wore a face-mask throughout the whole insanitary procedure of trimming my hair which made it difficult to ask him where he was going on his holidays this year. It would have been a poor joke in any case since the Chinese had no holidays at the time except a few days off for National Day, the Spring Festival and 1 May.

Lu Mei was fairly forthcoming on current fashions. She wore revolutionarily correct clothes at the Institute, favouring military khaki, which didn't do much for her rather sallow complexion, but she gave the impression that when she went home it was a rara skirt and to hell with it. We had a fairly complicated discussion, with diagrams, about a costume (and I can think of no better word) that she had ordered from the tailor. It involved a heart-shaped neckline and a full swirling skirt, all in black. She said that the year before, a few women had worn skirts of black silk, and that there would be more this year. But I felt that she moved in exalted circles and that we would not see many swirling skirts at the Languages Institute.

For us, the tailor was the gentleman at Wudaokou who specialized in target trousers. If you needed a patch on your trousers, you not only had to produce the trousers but also the patch (thus avoiding complications with cotton coupons, which the Wudaokou tailor was not authorized to accept). I once passed by the tailor's at the Friendship Store, an establishment that was far more on the ball, capable of copying Paris couture in locally made silk for diplomatic wives, but it was rather beyond my pocket. Inside there was a huge group of francophone Africans, with lots of children taking up all the seats. The cry came up from the tailor (through an interpreter), '*Où est Madame l'Ambassadrice?*' A small child bellowed in a voice that could be heard throughout the store, '*Madame l'Ambassadrice est allée pisser.*'

As the weather grew colder, we had to put on more layers. There was token heating in the dormitory block but none at all in the teaching block or anywhere else. Outside in the sun, it didn't feel too cold. Old men gathered together in the sunshine, sitting beneath the concrete plinths that stood at every street corner and that supported enormous slabs painted red and embellished with quotations from Chairman Mao. They wore black padded cotton jackets, black padded cotton trousers tied in at the ankles with black bindings, white socks and black cotton padded slippers. On their heads were great fur army hats, usually with the ear-flaps sticking up like rabbits' ears so that they could catch the drift of the conversation.

Indoors, it was another matter. Away from the warming sun, unheated classrooms with cold concrete floors seemed to gather and concentrate the cold. We had to resort to Chinese underwear which created a wardrobe upheaval. Chinese students wore two pairs of thin cotton track-suit trousers and a hand-knitted pair of long johns under their cotton trousers. As it was impossible to squeeze so many extra layers under our own tight trousers, we too had to buy baggy blue cotton trousers to accommodate the underwear. More cotton coupons.

A standard greeting in the winter was 'How many layers are you wearing?' In China most greetings were like that. As you entered the dormitory, the door-keeper, permanently established in a little glass-fronted booth to check on entrances and exits, would say, 'Are you coming in?' or, if you were leaving, 'Are you going out?' These statements of the obvious were sometimes irritating but the answer to 'How many layers are you wearing?' was often very surprising. It could be up to six. We rarely managed more than three and were invariably informed that we ought to Wear More or we would get ill.

The question was also often accompanied by a demonstration, carried out at ankle level. The track-suit trousers came in wonderful colours so that a blue cotton trouser leg might be discreetly rolled up to reveal a shocking pink track-suit on top of a sea-green layer. The top part of the body was another matter. No self-respecting girl would hang her underwear outside where men might see it, so my research into the subject was based on the washing-lines in the Institute washrooms. Starting next to the skin, a few girls wore bras. These were usually home-made and tended to flatten everything, rather like the inappropriately named 'liberty bodices'. They were made of cotton scraps, as were knickers, so they might be in pink gingham or curtain material with large flowers, or a patchwork of different pieces. On top of the bra went several track-suit tops and then a shirt. On top of that went a hand-knitted jumper. These were almost always striped, in a great variety of colours and wools. I discovered that these were washed once, in spring, after being completely unravelled. As they were separated from any source of body odour by several layers, their winter upkeep consisted of beating the dust out occasionally. When, one afternoon, I plunged a whole jumper into an enamel bowl full of White Cat detergent suds, a Chinese girl in the washroom screamed in horror. She explained that I should have unravelled it first, washed the resultant spaghetti and re-knitted it. She'd never seen me knitting. I would have frozen in the company of a number of doll's blankets.

As well as our heavy outer coats, we needed padded jackets. In order to save cotton coupons, I bought a silk wadded jacket and a large polyester jacket to cover it, both of these being expensive but made from unrationed materials. I could therefore wash the outer jacket if it got dirty, while the silk jacket was protected at the neck and cuffs by the outer jacket. People whose cuffs got a lot of wear also used to don sleeve-protectors, elasticated cotton tubes that stretched from wrist to elbow. Sitting at desks doing lessons, our cuffs were not subject to heavy-duty wear but the Canadian students acquired ostentatious sleeve-protectors to make them look more like worker-peasant-soldier students. I thought they looked like shop-girls.

If our cuffs survived classroom wear, restaurants were a different matter. Like the classrooms, restaurants were unheated. Sometimes, absolutely frozen after three hours of sitting still in an unheated classroom, we would rush off to the restaurant at Wudaokou and order a huge pile of *baozi*. These were large buns stuffed with meat, cabbage and onions, and, eaten with soy sauce and a little vinegar, they were very warming. They were, however, difficult enough to pick up and dip in soy sauce at the best of times, even if you had all your fingers free to manipulate the chopsticks. Eating them in an outer coat and padded cotton mittens was a very messy business, and it didn't take long for the front and cuffs of our coats to become stiff with soy sauce and bits of *baozi*.

First and Last Respects

Winter grew fiercer and the wind sometimes howled through the Languages Institute, sending all the bicycles crashing to the ground. We had an exam as a result of which four of us were found eligible to go on to Peking University to join a history class, though this did not happen overnight. Bureaucratic negotiations were to rumble on for several frustrating months. To pass the time before our transfer, we were given a different teacher and the content of our classes improved somewhat. *Elementary Chinese Book 2* was abandoned and we were now allowed to read actual texts. There was, however, a distinct shortage of decent reading matter as almost everything published between the beginning of time and 1966 was condemned as counter-revolutionary or worse. Even novels published in the 1950s, shortly after Liberation, were thought not to demonstrate a sufficiently clear class standpoint since they were littered with 'grey' characters who were neither out-and-out class enemies nor perfect Communist Party members.

In other media, it was sometimes possible to correct the class standpoint. Summoned to the Propaganda Tower, we were taken by bus to see a puppet show, much to the disgust of the more sophisticated among us. In fact, the puppets were wonderful, jointed wooden figures about two foot high manipulated with extraordinary skill. The story was very loosely based on a real event, when two little Mongolian sisters saved their collective's flock of sheep during a sudden blizzard, as a result of which they were terribly frostbitten, one of them losing one or both feet.

Even as a true story of infant heroism, the plot as it stood was not considered to be sufficiently clear on the matter of class. Though certainly not defined in atheist China as an act of God, weather was nevertheless class-less, so a class enemy puppet had to be introduced. Quite why a grey-faced landlord should be stalking the grasslands intent on destroying the collective and interfering with production was never explained. However, he withheld the weather forecast from the little girls. You could tell he was a class enemy because, on first appearance, he kicked a lamb.

Classical literature was thin on class enemies, but a few passages from Cao Xueqin's great eighteenth-century novel *Hongloumeng* (*Dream of the Red Chamber*, or *Story of the Stone*), passed the test, just. The novel describes the fortunes of a great household with its multiple family members and pretty servant girls, and their love affairs. None of this was of much use from a class standpoint, but fortunately Chapter 13 contains a section in which the riches of the family are described and we were allowed to read these isolated paragraphs.

Light relief continued to be provided by the Languages Institute. One afternoon in early December, the Chairman of the Revolutionary Committee of the Everest Climbing Team brought a film about their recent expedition and two of the climbers to the Institute. One of the mountaineers sat with his mouth hanging open and watched the film as if he was seeing Everest for the first time. The mountain was very beautiful. There were cosy shots of mountaineers at 26,000 feet, sitting in tiny tents and heating up tins of mandarin oranges. It was explained that the Chinese had tried to climb Everest in 1960 under the incorrect leadership of the capitalist-roader and arch-traitor Liu Shaoqi, then Chairman of the Communist Party. Everything, of course, went wrong. One climber had hallucinations, seeing Tibetan temples everywhere, so they had to send him to Lhasa to recuperate. Lhasa really is full of Tibetan temples, so I wondered how he got on. This time they had ascended the mountain under the correct leadership of Chairman Mao; indeed they said they would never have made it to the top had it not been for Chairman Mao and the Communist Party pointing the way. There was support from the people: from base camp at 19,000 feet came seventeen apples and a 'warm letter'. From 26,000 feet the climbers sent the apples back, saying 'Your need is as great as ours, take them back.' Wasting yet more valuable sherpa time and effort, base camp returned the fruit with yet another warm letter and the crew at 26,000 feet finally accepted the now rather bruised apples. 'Though they are small, we will put them into FULL PLAY in conquering the summit.'

Another exciting event at the busy 26,000-foot camp occurred when the only woman to get to the summit was accepted gloriously into the Communist Party and saluted the national flag, thereby establishing a world record for high-altitude political activity. As the Chinese had climbed without the benefit of oxygen, the dangers of brain damage were dramatically spelt out, leaving us in some doubt about the slack-jawed mountaineer beside us.

An impromptu visit to the Forbidden City took place

when we were invited to pay our last respects (and in my case, first respects, as I'd never heard of him) to Kang Sheng who had died at the age of seventy-seven. We were all rather keen to go as it meant escaping the China Knowledge class. A massive wreath of white tissue paper (white being the Chinese colour of mourning) and silver flowers on a flimsy bamboo stand was ordered on behalf of the students of the Languages Institute and with it we boarded the bus. We filed into the eastern side of the Forbidden City, the area where the emperors used to worship their ancestral tablets. All the green, red and gold walls were hung with black and yellow cloth in curving drapes and swags, and a snatch of the funeral march from *Saul* played continuously from tannoys hidden in the pine trees. With beautiful Albanian Arthur and another rather less glamorous Albanian holding our wreath, we marched into a hall where we shook hands with Chen Yonggui, the wrinkled head of the Dazhai production brigade whom we had last seen on a happier occasion in the New Summer Palace celebrating National Day, and with Wang Hairong, a small lady in a grey suit who was Mao's niece and Vice Foreign Minister.

We filed past a tiny casket and then, to my horror, were directed to shake hands with the Kang family. It seemed an awful intrusion. I was prepared for a lying-in-state but not for his tiny widow and tearful children. I felt marginally less intrusive when I was later informed by a furious German student that Kang Sheng had been head of the Secret Police for fifty years.

On Christmas Eve, Rose and I carolled our way across the diplomatic quarter. We had joined the British Embassy choir for the occasion. I always like singing loudly but I also had an ulterior motive. I wanted to see the Swiss Embassy which still occupied a traditional courtyard house next to the Forbidden City, and I knew the Swiss Embassy was on our itinerary. Though most of Peking's inhabitants lived in these little grey houses – a series of low buildings arranged around an open courtyard, usually with a large tree planted in the centre for summer shade – they were all but impenetrable to foreigners. Concealed behind high grey-brick walls, sometimes with a handsome red-painted, brass-handled double door, the interior was further screened from prying eyes by a brick 'spirit wall' just inside the front door. Ostensibly constructed to prevent the entrance of evil spirits who, it was believed, could only fly in straight lines, the spirit wall hid the courtyard from the outside world.

Ours was a serious choir, formed of diplomats, some of whom were very good singers, and beaten rather savagely into shape by the wife of the Head of Chancery in the British Embassy. We had to explain to Tian Laoshi that we needed to attend carol practice every Thursday evening and that it often went on so long that we could not always get back the same night and might therefore be late for classes on Friday mornings. To our surprise, he took it very well and tended to smile and wink whenever our absence was mentioned. It transpired that he assumed that since I was the oldest and a sort of 'class mother', and Rose was a very reliable citizen, we had been appointed to report back to the Embassy on a weekly basis. This was what the Chinese would have done, so it seemed quite normal to him. We, however, were rather embarrassed at the suggestion. Instead of low-level espionage we were learning complicated carols. We had to include Sibelius for the Finns and a rather wonderful French carol, '*Il est né le divin enfant, jouez hautbois, résonnez musettes*', for the French. There was also Berlioz's 'Three kings from di-i-istant lands afar' with a solo by the

Australian First Secretary which was a triumph from an
unlikely quarter.

During the weeks of rehearsals, Rose and I were directed
to sleep overnight every Thursday in an Embassy flat that
was being redecorated. Donning vast pink winceyette night-
ies, thoughtfully provided by our mothers for the cold winter
nights, we slept on mattresses in the empty apartment. On
the first Friday morning, we went into the kitchen to make a
cup of coffee. There we found four Chinese house-painters
brewing up and rolling cigarettes. The sight of two English
ladies in giant pink nightdresses drove them to work. Once
dressed (a lengthy business in winter) we went round the
corner to a carter's roadside caff for breakfast. It served
soup, thick with onions and beancurd, and *youtiaor*, long
deep-fried salty doughnut-like things, to dip into the soup.
Our fellow-breakfasters were cheerful peasants with brown
weather-beaten faces, wearing long coats of curly
Mongolian lamb, with the fur on the inside, and the usual
army fur hats with rabbit ears sticking up. Outside, the mules
and donkeys, still harnessed to long, low vegetable carts,
breathed out hot clouds of breath as they ate from their
nose-bags. Most of them had a cloth slung beneath their
tails, to catch droppings. In line with the general obsession
with manure, these nappies prevented any loss of the valuable fertilizer.

Unaccustomed to gracious living, we found the travelling
carol performance on Christmas Eve a revelation. The Swiss
Embassy, however, was rather a disappointment. Its courtyards had been covered over and its rooms were small and
cramped. The Sibelius went down well at the Finnish
Embassy. As we sang 'Be still my heart', the Ambassador, a
somewhat sinister figure, six foot seven inches tall and
wearing dark glasses, could be seen wiping a tear from under

his shades. At the French Embassy, the audience sat on tiny little gilt chairs with red velvet seats and we were served champagne. We ate cinnamon biscuits shaped like stars and hearts at the Dutch Embassy and ended up drinking beer with the Australians.

On Christmas Day, we were invited to the Embassy. We said prayers and the Ambassador read the lesson from an eagle-shaped lectern that had been rescued from the Boxers in 1900 (bullet-holes still visible). The wife of the Councillor

played the piano and the Ambassador taught us how to dance eightsome reels. All the while, silent Chinese servants in white jackets padded past hysterical guests in evening clothes who were skipping about and eating mince-pies.

On Boxing Day, we were again invited by the Embassy, this time to the New Summer Palace where it snowed. It was a magical sight: all the red and blue pavilions had white roofs, and the snow-covered slopes of Longevity Hill merged with the vast iced lake, white against the grey sky. Owing to the cold, the whole area was almost completely deserted, except for British residents clustered on the frozen lake. The First Secretary zipped about on skates, offering hot punch out of thermos flasks. What with the slightly uneven surface, he dropped three and broke them. I thought about how cold it was beneath us and wondered how much hot punch he needed to spill before the entire British community joined the frozen fish. Tom, an art history graduate from Oxford, discovered that a complete beginner could skate quite fearlessly when wearing Chinese padded trousers and jacket. Falling over didn't hurt at all though you did need the assistance of a lot of people to get you up again. Rose and I walked across the frozen lake to an island. We were followed all the way by three People's Liberation Army soldiers but when the ice boomed, they disappeared like rabbits. Lei Feng would not have run away.

As part of its great kindness to us, the Embassy offered all the British students the opportunity to stay for the holidays in the empty flat Rose and I had slept in after carol practice. It was still bare of furniture but was now heated to tropical temperatures. Though I welcomed the warmth, I was less happy to find that the kitchen was full of basking cockroaches. After three days, I retreated to the Languages Institute where it was much too cold for cockroaches. There I found a message instructing me to collect a Christmas cake sent from home. It had already made an abortive journey to Paris where its would-be courier was refused a visa, so it had had to be sent back to Heathrow and was now awaiting my attention at the China Airlines office in the centre of town.

Cycling in winter was hard because the cold air hurt when you breathed it in. The hardy wore face-masks, the weak took a bus. The bus was, as usual, overfull. Bus travel was

much more difficult in winter since, what with all their layers
and padding, everyone was at least twice as fat. But the
padding did have one advantage. If you just managed to get
on to the bottom step of the bus, the conductress would
come round and place a foot firmly in the middle of your
back, forcing you inwards so that the doors could close. This
was less painful in winter although it added a series of dusty
footprints to the back of a coat whose front was already liberally decorated with soy sauce.

The bus conductress was having a bad day. I bought a
ticket because I was far too conspicuous to get away with not
doing so, but many others avoided her. She rounded on a
lady who was holding a thickly padded baby and who tried to
explain that she couldn't get her purse out without dropping
the baby. She was right to hang on because the buses generally cornered on two wheels, although this particular bus was
so tightly packed that the baby would probably have been
buoyed up even without being held. She escaped punishment but a ticketless young man was chased down the road,
caught, returned to the bus and held prisoner all the way to
the terminus with the conductress shouting that he had the
heart of a wolf and the lungs of a dog.

My Christmas cake was handed to me in a white cotton
pillow-case. It had turned into a loose mass of crumbs
which I had to reconstitute. In the evening I went to a hot-
pot restaurant near the Old Summer Palace with Thomas
and Michael, two German students. The Old Summer Palace
was much more romantic than the New Summer Palace. It
had once been a glorious sight, a mixture of traditional
Chinese gardens with red-pillared pavilions, piles of eccen-
tric rocks and pools, and 'European' palaces, built for the
Qianlong Emperor in the eighteenth century by a series of
Jesuit artists and engineers. The great painter Giuseppe

Castiglione, famous for his portraits of the Emperor's greyhounds, horses and hunting expeditions, assisted Father
Sichelbarth with designs for Classical buildings with rusti-
cated stonework and columns wreathed in swags of carved
stone flowers and foliage. Another priest, Father Benoist,
designed a massive fountain where stone animals (the twelve
animals of the Chinese twelve-year cycle that also represented the twelve 120-minute 'hours' in the traditional
Chinese day) spouted water in their turn into a great shell-
shaped basin. All this elaboration was described in one
Chinese guidebook as 'Barock' and in others as 'Jesuit colo-
nial architecture'.

In 1860, during the Second Opium War, British and
French troops looted and destroyed much of the Old
Summer Palace, leaving only some romantic ruins which
included a few flower-swagged columns and the great shell-
shaped basin of the fountain. It was a wonderful place to
walk for it was almost always deserted except for a few peasants tending their lotus plants in the now-abandoned pools.

Beside the Old Summer Palace was a village, no more than
a cluster of small houses and wooden-fronted shops, and a
little restaurant. There the three of us sat down at a central
table with the other diners. The table was built round a stove,
on top of which was a circular trough. In it you dropped
wafer-thin slices of mutton, spring onions and cabbage. The
resulting mixture turned into a rich soup from which you
then had to try to retrieve your bits of meat and cabbage. As
I sat with my trousers singeing against the stove, Thomas
explained why he had come to China: 'I have the basements
of Leninismus in my pocket and I am making revolution.'

On New Year's Eve, there was another highly coloured
tea-party at the Institute with more bright yellow lemonade,
peanuts, meringues, cheese biscuits and sugar-coated potato

crisps, all piled in tottering mounds on our plates by Fu Laoshi, Tian Laoshi and Hu Laoshi. There were performances. We sang 'Old MacDonald Had a Farm' once again (we were by now rather good at it). In the evening, there was a real party given by the German students who served Chinese champagne. They were generous, although they could afford to push the collective boat out now and then for they received huge student allowances from the German government. Apparently, the student rates for famously expensive Japan had also been applied to China, owing to geographical proximity and in the face of political and economic differences. The effect of champagne and a general shortage of women made some of the Muslim students slightly tricky but we managed to remain on cheerful terms. The French girls were less cheerful. They had been informed that if they wanted to go to university, they would have to go to Shenyang in the permafrost of the Dongbei (Manchuria) because the Peking and Shanghai universities claimed to be full. With the cold wind howling outside and bicycles crashing to the ground, going further north was a frightening prospect.

Two Poems and Another Funeral

The dust that was blown into every crevice by the freezing wind had got into my cassette-recorder which began to make alarming noises. Life without music was almost unthinkable so I tried to get it repaired. I went to the centre of town, to Wangfujing ('The Well of the Princely Mansion') where Communism had cast its pall over the department stores. They were great dusty buildings with huge dusty windows filled with displays of carefully arranged pyramids of dusty beer bottles and little dusty brown bakelite televisions arranged on dusty silk sheets. Inside they were poorly lit and their layout was difficult to understand. Cloth shoes were sold separately from leather and plastic shoes, which were on a completely different floor, and ceramic cups and plates were separated from enamel mugs and bowls. There were a large number of assistants, mostly engaged in conversation with each other when they weren't arguing with shoppers. Owing to the general lack of money, the purchase of any item, even one as small as a plastic soap-dish, took hours and hours, with the shopper carefully examining each proffered soap-dish for faults and the shop assistant whipping them away as soon as they were placed to one side, making comparison even more difficult in the dim light.

I did find a shop in Wangfujing that sold cassette-recorders but it did not repair them. 'Go north,' said the shop assistant. Peking residents have a built-in compass which is reinforced by the regular grid of the streets that, almost without exception, run north–south or east–west. (When I helped the Chinese girl in the next room at the Institute to move her wardrobe, she kept telling me to lift up the south side.) I went north along Wangfujing, eventually finding a sign that said 'Electrical repairs this way.' I headed off down the tiny back streets, wondering if this was where ambassadors brought their toasters and curling-tongs. The grey walls of the low courtyard houses concealed their interiors and on a cold evening with the sun sinking fast there was no one about. I knocked on the door of a courtyard house and went in. The courtyard was full of children and potted chrysanthemums and rusty wire. An old man in one of the wings lay asleep on a brick bed.

Eventually a young man was summoned by the children and, though he said he only repaired turbines and dynamos, he gave me tea and told me where to go. It was good to be sat down and talked to in the courtyard. As foreign students we had so little communication with ordinary people and such a sense of otherness that exchanging platitudes whilst perched on an oil-can was a ridiculously heart-warming experience.

The great excitement of the New Year was the publication in the *People's Daily* of two poems by Chairman Mao which had been written in 1965. They were not his best efforts but every single student in the Languages Institute wished to translate them into English so I dealt with a stream of earnest visitors bearing versions which invariably skirted over the rather rough language of one of the poems. It was about a great bird stretching its wings in flight. Looking down it saw cities where bullets were flying and where the ground was covered with bomb craters. A sparrow in a bramble bush was terrified. The huge bird asked the sparrow where it thought it could go to escape and the sparrow replied, 'I will go to the Jade Palace of the fairies in the mountain' (which was officially glossed as the Kremlin). The huge bird said, 'But haven't you seen the three-family treaty signed two years ago in the brightness of autumn?' (which we were told referred to nuclear non-proliferation treaties which the Chinese regarded as pointless as long as stock-piling continued). 'But', said the sparrow, 'there is always plenty to eat there, boiled potatoes and meat, for example.' (The Chinese described Khrushchev's Communism as Potatoes and Meat Communism.) The huge bird then said, in effect, 'You don't need to fart to see which way the world is going.' The last sentence was invariably translated as 'Don't talk windy nonsense; look at the real changes in the world' and nothing I said could alter it.

The other poem was more straightforwardly poetic, about revisiting the scenes of great battles of the mid-1930s during the civil war against Chiang Kai-shek in the mountains of Jiangxi province. It ended with an injunction to 'Climb the nine mountains and catch the moon; swim the five oceans and capture turtles. Nothing is impossible if you stand up and clench your fist.' This was 1976's New Year instruction, written on strips of red paper and pasted beside the door of every house.

As negotiations progressed with Peking University over our transfer, lessons continued at the Institute. We were taken to a middle (secondary) school which had huge classes of up to fifty students all sitting at rows of desks with their hands behind their backs. As part of the Revolution in Education, a worker taught a physics lesson. Under the Revolution in Education guidelines, it was better to be 'red' than 'expert' (combinations were disallowed), so the class had to be severely practical. He taught them all about broadcasting and tannoys. Tannoys were everywhere in China. Every innocent tree concealed a black trumpet and each one of the sparse street-lights had a tannoy fixed to it; and they all broadcast the official government radio programmes all the time. Inside places like the Languages Institute, there was a department that produced its own radio programmes carefully timed to accommodate the official government radio broadcasts. Prize-winning essays were read out on the Languages Institute tannoys. I was terribly embarrassed when my account of open-door schooling was selected. It took a bit of editing, with Tian Laoshi adding all sorts of firm political messages that I had failed to include, but to my horror it was broadcast. I needn't have worried: as the tannoys emitted political messages all day and every day, no one, anywhere in China, ever paid any attention.

Though the physics lesson was quite efficient, it was faintly depressing to think that fifty more eager-beavers would now be able to go out and set up yet more tannoys in the trees. After the physics lesson I read aloud to an English class. The text was about wicked Soviet revisionists making veteran workers redundant but thereby 'picking up stones only to drop them on their own feet' (English idiom).

Afterwards, Beth and I went for a walk. We both enjoyed periodically escaping from the masses. That afternoon we discovered the narrow street that runs from the Temple of Confucius to what had once been the Confucian Academy. Every sizeable town in China had had its Temple of

Confucius, but that in Peking, rebuilt by the Wanli Emperor in the late sixteenth century and then again by the Qianlong Emperor in the late eighteenth century, was one of the most important. Its courtyards and buildings housed stelae recording all the names of those who had passed the bureaucratic examinations (based on the Confucian classics) which admitted them to service in the imperial government. The Academy next door had been the College for the Sons of the Nation since 1404. Now both were firmly shut in case evil

influences should emerge, their tantalizing yellow-roofed halls and ancient trees, providing refuge for tannoy-deafened sparrows, just visible above the grey walls. The street on which they stood was quiet and elegant, with tall trees and a series of *pailou* or ornamental arches bearing fading gold, green, red and blue painted patterns. These handsome timber gateways, erected at major crossroads, used to be common in Peking, but I was told that most of them had been moved to Taoranting Park in the 1950s so I made a special trip there one afternoon. The park was quite pleasant but was clearly a modern municipal creation for it contained nothing old. I asked about the *pailou* at the gate but met with absolute incomprehension. Eventually an elderly woman was summoned who remembered the *pailou* but told me that they had all been chopped up, leaving those outside the Confucian temple as Peking's sole representatives.

In a tiny stationery shop around the corner from what had once been the educational heart of China, presided over by the memory of Confucius, we bought some amazing plastic pencil sharpeners in the shape of swans and the circular, blue-roofed Temple of Heaven where the emperors kept their ancestral tablets. All inventive design appeared to be concentrated in the plastics industry.

After another bus-ride from hell (when I feared that, as in *The Third Policeman*, I was so close to a PLA soldier that we would exchange atoms and identities), we had a funny supper with the local residents of our Friendship Class, those who had not gone off to join their families for the Spring Festival elsewhere. They told us they called us 'thermos flasks' because we were cold outside but warm within. They also said that we looked old in our twenties but young in middle age, whereas they described themselves as looking very young when young and very old when old.

On 8 January, Zhou Enlai died. The atmosphere over the next couple of weeks was one of unmitigated gloom and occasional hysteria. On the first morning, our teacher came into class in tears. The Chinese side of the dining-room was normally bedlam, with tin spoons bashing tin bowls and much cheerful screaming and spitting of fish-bones and bits of gristle on to the table-top, but now it fell silent. A middle-aged lady called Li from our Friendship Class grabbed me to tell me the news. I said how sorry I was and she clasped me and wept. We later decided she was something of a ghoul because she went on clasping people and weeping for more than five days and trapped me on the stairs to ask about the memorial meeting which we had been compelled to attend: 'Were many people in tears?'

We had submitted to the usual whip-round for a wreath to take to the memorial meeting. The same halls, to the east of the Forbidden City, were more sombre than they had been at Kang Sheng's memorial and everyone was weeping noisily. While we were queuing to file in, Beth felt faint, a physical condition rather admired by the sobbing crowds who assumed she was even more overcome than they were. I ushered her back to the bus to lie down. In front of Zhou Enlai's urn, the rest of us were lined up, with Arthur in the front row, thank goodness, as she was so striking and sobbed so dramatically. Blinding television lights flashed again and again while our grief-stricken teachers practically screamed in front of the tiny urn. We shook hands with Mao's niece, again, and Chen Yonggui, again. He was crying, the tears running like streams through the gullies of his wrinkled face.

Beth had a quieter time listening to the bus drivers gloomily discussing the future now that the only leader who had had a calming effect on the population was gone. Though he must have outdone Machiavelli in remaining close to Mao and surviving, he had managed to radiate charm, even at a distance. All the foreign leaders who met him, from Georges Pompidou to Edward Heath, testified to his attraction, and he was clearly equally effective at home. If the silk-workers of Hangzhou went on strike and civil turmoil threatened, the Central Committee of the Communist Party only had to dispatch Zhou Enlai on a plane for things to settle down immediately. The bus drivers gloomily concluded that there was no 'leadership' left. They didn't mention Deng Xiaoping who lacked Zhou's charisma, or Mao who was rumoured to be speechless and nearly lifeless.

When we got back to the Institute, the television room, normally as empty as a deconsecrated private chapel because the television programmes were so awful, was stuffed to bursting with Chinese students watching us file past the urn and all screaming and moaning. All day long for a week the tannoy broadcast nothing except the telegrams of condolence which were arriving from all corners of the world. The British telegram was very late and was not included in the front-rank group but was broadcast days later along with those of São Tomé and Paraguay. Apparently the Embassy had been thrown into confusion by Harold Wilson's message which began, 'I first met Zhou Enlai in Geneva in 1953.' The Indo-China conference to which he referred had actually taken place in 1954 so they had had to telephone backwards and forwards endlessly before the telegram could be delivered.

Everybody in Peking wore a black armband and nobody smiled; it was as if everybody's father had died at the same time. After a week, I felt like reminding them that Chairman Mao had said, 'Turn grief into strength.' I had my own problems. As there was an uneven number of English females and I was the oldest, I had so far had a two-bedded room to myself. This meant that I could decide when the light went out and didn't have to chat endlessly, although it also meant rather more Chinese visitors wanting me to polish their translations of poems. Suddenly, in the midst of this darkest mourning, a new batch of Australian and New Zealand students arrived. There was only one New Zealand girl and she was assigned to share my room.

Deepest Cold

Keri was tall, very fair and very pretty but also inordinately intense. Two weeks after Zhou's death when, officially, the country was supposed to have got back to normal, the New Zealand Ambassador invited all the students to dine. Keri, who had arrived too late for the memorial service but had thrown herself into the weeping and howling sessions in the television room with the best of them, was outraged. 'How can he even think of it?' she demanded. 'How can we think of enjoying ourselves after this tragedy? I'm sure the Chinese will be terribly shocked.' I pointed out that mourning was officially over and that the New Zealand Ambassador, mindful of the dangers of football games and highly trained in protocol, was hardly likely to do anything rash, and anyway the food would be good and there would be wine. Her compromise was to go but to wear her darkest clothes and keep her black armband on in order to cast as much gloom as possible on the proceedings.

Keri was keen to throw herself into Chinese politics. She should have shared a room with one of the Canadian Marxist-Leninists but there was none to spare. She was

terribly gratified when I told her I'd seen a Chinese map of
the world's potential revolutionary uprisings marked with
flames and that there had been a huge fire practically obliter-
ating New Zealand. This was due to over-optimistic reports
from the leader of the New Zealand Maoist Party (a very
small group that had broken away from the old Communist
Party and which, anywhere else, might have been called splittist) and bore little relation to the truth as far as I could tell,
but Keri felt that it gave her status. She became very close to
the Canadians and was invited to join a study group in which
they read *Das Kapital* and other Marxist classics under the
guidance of a couple of long-term residents, one from a
China missionary background. Both were redder than red.
As we had an awful lot of Marx and Lenin not to mention
Engels and Stalin in class, I found it hard to understand how
anyone could take any more. But it got her out of our room
on Saturday evenings.

Her presence also prompted me to start exploring more
of the city, just to get away. It was frustrating but also exhil-
arating. Almost nothing was open, but glimpses behind gates
or over brick walls were always to be hoped for. In the south,
near where the *pailou* had been chopped up in Taoranting
Park, were two huge enclosures. One was the Temple of
Heaven, where the emperors had arrived in procession just
before the Chinese New Year to worship their ancestral
tablets, report to their ancestors on the year's events and
offer prayers and sacrifices for the coming year. The great
round halls with their cone-shaped, blue-tiled roofs and
rows of tall pine trees planted in serried rows were visible
from outside the enclosing wall though the complex was
closed to all but special visitors like American Presidents.

Just across the road was the enclosure of the former Altar
of Agriculture where the emperors had made a similar trip,

just after the New Year, to initiate the agricultural year by ploughing a ceremonial furrow. I explored Peking carrying Arlington and Lewisohn's 1935 guidebook, *In Search of Old Peking*, in which, bemoaning the changes already apparent in 1935, either Arlington or Lewisohn said gloomily, 'I expect that any minute now, the Temple of Heaven will become a stadium or a swimming-pool.' He was almost right, for though the Temple of Heaven was intact, if closed, the Altar of Agriculture enclosure now housed both a swimming-pool and a stadium.

One freezing Sunday, we went in the Embassy minibus on an hour-long drive northwards to the Great Wall. It was lovely, even in minus 10 degrees and with a rough north wind sweeping over the mountains. All the waterfalls looked as if they had frozen instantly for the ice hung in waves and curls, and the bed of the stream below was quite dry. We stopped at the pass of Badaling, where the old road north ran through a huge gate in the Great Wall. The wall we saw had been faced with brick during the Ming and restored many times since, transforming the original *pisé* or stamped-earth construction which dated back nearly 2,000 years. Many walls had been built in China over the centuries, indeed Chinese society resembled nothing so much as walls within walls, both mental and physical, but the Great Wall, maintained to keep the northern barbarians out, had never been very effective. Still, seen from Badaling, where the two wings snaked upwards from the gate and ran over the bare hillsides into the infinite distance, it was a wonderful sight.

There were a few brave Chinese families crawling up to the top with us, all battling hysterically against the freezing wind. We had to climb almost vertical slopes with the wind suddenly knocking us sideways and then dropping as we crept past the battlements. On the way down, we passed a group of woodcutters, all wearing tattered padded clothes with the stuffing escaping so that they looked like so many figures in a Bruegel painting. Their bicycles were piled high with bundles of wood. When they set off down the road, nothing was visible except great piles of sticks, like runaway haystacks rolling down the hill. Afterwards, we went to skate on the reservoir by the Ming tombs.

The reservoir was glassy and extraordinary to skate on, being green and full of bubbles in white spirals like Venetian millefiori or streaked with rock-crystal wisps. If you listened with your ear close to the cold surface, you could hear the ice cracking and the water rushing below.

Another day German Thomas and I bicycled to the beautiful village behind the Old Summer Palace. The main street was lined with little timber-framed shops, like houses turned inside out but with more windows of very elegant lattice work. In the side streets between the houses, pigs in their sties all had their noses burrowed well into the straw. This, according to traditional Chinese folklore, otherwise known as stating the obvious and retailed in our class textbooks, was a sure indication that the weather was very cold.

In fact the weather in Peking is very predictable. A raw wind full of dust from Siberia had been blowing when we went to the Great Wall. Such a wind always presaged a period of intense cold which the pigs had noticed too. We followed lots of mules and donkeys along the main road and, in turn, were followed by lots of small boys. They asked where we were from, so we told them and they looked utterly blank. We then explained that Germany and England were in Europe (Ouzhou). One small geographer caught the general drift and began to chant, 'Ouzhou, Meizhou [America], Feizhou [Africa], Yazhou [Asia]'.

Behind the houses there was one interesting building with
a two-storey pavilion behind it. As we turned into a maze of
lanes to get nearer I tried to enthuse Thomas with the detail
of the timber and stucco work, but then we realized that we
were standing in someone's front garden and that their goat
was getting edgy.

In the days around the Spring Festival, we were at something of a loose end. For a few days, shops shut and families
gathered together to make dumplings stuffed with pork and

cabbage, eat sunflower seeds and visit their neighbours,
bearing gifts of dried fruit and more sunflower seeds. In the
narrow lanes of the villages surrounding the Languages
Institute, families shuffled in and out of their neighbours'
houses, quiet in their cotton-soled shoes, and the only sound
of merriment was the thundering of fire-crackers let off in
the evening to frighten away evil spirits.

The students who lived outside Peking were allowed to go

home for a fortnight so classes ground to a halt. Cultural activities, however, were not neglected. We were privileged to attend an early viewing of the first film about the Revolution in Education which was attractively titled *Rupture* or *Split* (indicating some disagreement amongst the authoritative English translators) and which caricatured experts along Gradgrind lines. Despite their startlingly frail physiques, grey faces and stupid, impractical views on life, these capitalist-roaders actually managed to gain control of the University in the absence of heroic President Long. He returned, a one-man cavalry, and routed them. Hooray.

At a similar loose end, our Friendship Class paid us several visits. I told Mrs Zhou and the other ladies how to win the pools and how to bet on greyhounds. Though I had no personal experience of either my granny did do the pools. I also gave them an outline of contemporary English society and drew a double-decker bus. In Peking some buses were twice as long as usual with a rubber concertina in the middle and a sort of swivelling platform in the centre which was quite fun to stand on, and others had little buses hitched on behind with a separate conductress.

Hu Laoshi came to visit and found only Rose and me in. We sat in Rose's room eating sunflower seeds which reminded us of hamsters. I told him about my hamster called Phoebe, who had been born rather grandly in the Vicarage of St Martin-in-the-Fields *circa* 1965, and how she was forever escaping, taking up noisy residence in the piano, and in the washing-machine where she made a nest by chewing the fringe from the rug in the hall. Hamsters originated in the Gobi desert but they were quite unknown in Peking, as were pet-shops, an idea that made Hu Laoshi's eyes bulge. Paying for a rat? In China people kept crickets and wild birds in tiny cages but cats and dogs were definitely workers. You could, apparently, eat dog in two restaurants in Peking but the Germans, having boldly ordered 'red-stewed dog', lost their nerve at the last minute.

After two months of lengthy arguments about whether we could or could not go, Peking University suddenly demanded yet more exams. There was an oral which Beth and I sat together. She got confused between line struggles and class conflicts and I waved my arms as if the exam was in semaphore. Semaphore or not, we passed and were told we would move after the Spring Festival which gave us time to arrange a trip to Datong with the Austrians and some of the German students. Datong, in Shanxi province, was famous for its series of cave-temples with Buddhist carvings dating back to the mid-fourth century. It was also only about eight hours west of Peking by train, a one-stop trip, for which only one travel permit was required.

Armed with our permits, we travelled overnight on hard seats. It was fortunate that the train was not full because though there were officially three seats on the narrow benches, what with our giant winter padded coats, there was hardly room for two European bottoms. We slept with our heads cradled in our arms on the tables. When we arrived in the early morning, the air in Datong was so thick with coal dust that you could crunch it on your teeth. Every little house had a small coal stove and the production of several thousand breakfasts filled the air with a thick smog. The Chinese students automatically referred to London as Wu Du (Smog Capital) and no amount of lecturing about Clean Air Acts could dislodge the title. Morning in Datong brought back childhood memories of the (pre-Clean Air Act) yellow smog that tasted very similar though less crunchy.

After breakfast, we went out through the dry yellow hills

along a frozen river-bed to the Yungang caves. Cut into a long yellow cliff above the river-bed, the hundreds of small dark caves looked like the holes in Gruyère cheese. At the centre was a huge Buddha, 130 feet high, once concealed by a building but now exposed to the cold air. Each cave was filled with carved Buddhas cut in the soft yellow-grey sandstone. In the 1,000-Buddha cave were thousands of tiny identical figures carved in little niches. In another cave there were lovely bas-reliefs of scenes from the life of the Buddha showing him setting off from little Chinese buildings and wearing Chinese clothes.

In between the caves was a wooden structure, built almost into the cliff, that protected some rather garish painted Buddhist figures that had clearly been restored very recently. The stairs were difficult (with one half step per foot) and the balconies were rickety, but if you braved them you could stand close to the eaves where wind-bells tinkled in the cold wind.

The village nearby was very poor. The houses were made of the same yellow earth as the walls and the outbuildings so that everything seemed half-buried, part of the earth. But the windows and interiors were cheerful and much better than grey Peking. At the Spring Festival they repaired the windows and put up new sheets of window paper painted in bright colours with flowers and birds and cats. Inside, the walls and the smelly oil-cloth that covered the *kang*, or brick bed, were decorated with shiny flowers and fruit and patterns so that the room looked quite East European. Every family had one, or even two, cats. As cats were regarded as workers, their presence suggested plagues of mice and rats.

The next day we were taken down a coal mine in so much protective clothing that it was hardly possible to move. We had to put on one thin track-suit, one very thick one, denim overalls, a vast padded waistcoat, an enormous helmet with a headlamp, mine so big it kept falling over my face, and wellington boots. In deference to our vast Western proportions, each item was outsize, especially the wellington boots. Our guides were worried that we might fall over as we waded through black water, crawled up 10,000 steps and clambered over coal heaps, but my boots were so enormous I could hardly walk at all. It was surprisingly warm below ground and interesting to stumble along endless black tunnels and see flickering lights ahead. We went to the coal face. Contrary to my expectations, it was huge, a great, dusty Albert Hall filled with the thin beams of headlamps and men shovelling. German Thomas said it was a very easy mine to work: with such huge seams of coal they could use dynamite to loosen it, an idea I did not much like when so far underground.

Then, utterly filthy, we went back past the huge yellow city walls (of pounded earth, like our summer greenhouses) to two wonderful temples in the centre of the town. The Lower Temple had been constructed in 1038 and housed a group of Buddhist figures of extreme elegance, leaning forward in front of a library that lined the walls, built of timber, like a miniature suspended palace. In the Upper Temple was a massive hall, said to date back to the twelfth century. Its interior columns were huge and the walls were over a yard thick to keep out the intense cold and freezing winter winds which rang the wind-bells endlessly. Though the interior itself and its massive Buddha figures were sombre and elegant, the walls were painted with incredibly garish frescoes of Buddhist grotesques, executed by a local painter, Dong An, at the end of the nineteenth century and very much to the popular taste. The bus-driver said to me, 'You'll like this one, it's much better than those old caves.'

On the train back to Peking we passed dozens of little villages. In those near Datong each house had bright painted window papers with cats and birds in celebration of the New Year, but as we drew further away, they were replaced by little red paper-cuts, silhouetted against the clean white paper. I discovered from the Germans that they did not have a continuous present tense but they informed me that 'We are finding it such an attractive proposition that when we are speaking English we are using it all the time.' I told Michael how surprised Hu Laoshi had been by my stories of the hamsters that we kept in such unimaginable luxury in our homes and he said, 'Yes, and they are not even making eggs.'

The Institute took us on a last (compulsory) trip, this time to Shijiazhuang, the Crewe of China. Shijiazhuang lies not far south of Peking, its sole tourist attraction the Norman Bethune Hospital for War, Peace and Revolution (I may have got one of those wrong). Norman Bethune (1881–1938) was a Canadian doctor who made a significant contribution to thoracic surgery and who went to serve in Spain during the civil war. There he pioneered the use of mobile blood transfusion and surgical units at the front. He arrived in China in 1938 intending to introduce the same methods but unfortunately cut himself whilst operating and died of septicaemia the same year. His grave, and that of an Indian, Dr Kotnis, who had also volunteered to work with the Red Army, had been moved from more distant parts to Shijiazhuang for the convenience of visitors using the rail network.

In the hospital, stoical Chinese patients were operated on for the removal of goitres and tonsils with acupuncture as the only form of analgesia and a lot of foreign students peering at them. Gerry had been forbidden to come on the hospital visit for fear of accidents and I hung back behind the door. Keri was right at the front, joggling the surgeon's arm and exclaiming loudly that this was the only way to do it.

The rest of the day was taken up with an exceptionally repetitive session in which doctor after doctor told us that analgesia by acupuncture was the poor countries' answer to ridiculously expensive (expert, ivory-towerist) Western surgery and that it took only a few weeks to learn how to do it. Then nurse after nurse came in and told us how they had learned from the spirit of Dr Norman Bethune. 'I was going out to play basketball when I noticed a patient dying. My first instinct was to go out and play basketball but then I thought to myself, what would Norman Bethune have done? I concluded that he would not have gone out to play basketball so I performed an emergency tracheotomy and saved the patient's life.' I amused myself by translating for a group of francophone Africans. Their Chinese vocabulary might not have been up to major surgery but they did know how the Chinese translated revolutionary concepts into French and regarded it as a whole new way of perverting the language. They taught me the correct French forms, like '*apprendre à*' or '*prendre l'exemple sur*' for useful phrases like 'learn from' as in 'learn from Norman Bethune'.

Not a University but a Thermometer

The Spring Festival had a bad effect on the Albanian students, and the Languages Institute became a battlefield. Fireworks must have been banned in Tirana because in Peking the Albanian students were quite uncontrollable, blowing up milk bottles, exploding African students and generally thundering. The air was thick with gunpowder fumes. More picturesque, though unappealing to the Albanians, was the sight of children in the evenings carrying great round red paper lanterns with candles inside, bobbing about in fields and lanes, welcoming the New Year.

With the end of the Spring Festival it was time for Beth and me to move to Peking University. We were quite sad to pack up and leave the Languages Institute (though quite glad to say goodbye to Keri). Lots of people came to see us off in a snowstorm, including an Albanian who was very helpful loading bags on to the bus but who then gave us an Albanian send-off by viciously hurling snowballs at the windows.

Peking University was huge, with more than 7,000 students who knew it as Beida (a contraction of its Chinese name, Beijing Daxue). It had a nice pagoda which was actually a water-tower and lots of crumbling Chinese-style buildings designed by an architect from Yale called Henry Killam Murphy. They had only been built at the turn of the century but lack of upkeep left them looking venerable. Some of them hummed as they housed computers and atom-splitters. The campus, developed in the early years of the twentieth century as Yanjing University, an American missionary foundation, occupied a site which had previously been the country estate of Heshen, the Qianlong Emperor's favourite, a man who had also inhabited the Gongwangfu, a mansion in the Houhai area of the city. The Gongwangfu was another of the many buildings that I circled on my bike, riding round and round the outer walls, hoping to see something of the sumptuous interior, but like the rest it was firmly closed. Lord Macartney, who led the first British embassy to China in 1792–4, had stayed at Heshen's country estate and must have seen some of the same ponds, rockeries and small lodges at the northern end of the University campus.

I had a lovely room in the female foreigners' dormitory just inside the south-east gate which looked out on to a snow-covered bank and through trees to the playing-fields beyond and the south wall of the University. On the other side of the wall, carters parked their donkeys as they took lunch at the Long March Restaurant on the far side of the road. A donkey that had finished its nose-bag could make a truly unearthly noise until you got used to it. The room was larger than my old one at the Languages Institute and there was the promise of a real Chinese room-mate at the end of the month.

On our first morning, classes consisted of Chinese history from seven-thirty for two hours and then Chinese language until lunch at eleven-thirty. For all our history lectures, we joined a *jinxiuban* or vocational class in Chinese history which had been set up to allow local workers to improve their historical knowledge in order to sharpen their propaganda work. The students were mostly in their late twenties and the majority were workers from nearby factories. There were also three People's Liberation Army soldiers (one female) but we were rather thin on peasants. The addition of foreign students to the class was something of a mixed blessing. Those foreign students who studied literature or philosophy (Marxism-Leninism-Mao Zedong Thought) had separate classes in which the content level could be minimally adjusted to European views but our history teachers, mindful of the dangers of accusations of 'expertise' or bourgeois liberalism from the Chinese students, made few concessions. They wrote new terms and names on the blackboard for us, and that was all.

Life was more spartan at Beida. To fill our thermoses, we had to stomp off through the snow to the canteen, which made me feel like Nature, abhorring vacuums. There was a bare hour of heating in the dormitories in the morning and evening but none during the day and none at all in the classrooms.

The showers were truly communal so I got a further glimpse of some very Victorian Chinese underwear. Added to the lack of individual showers was a tighter regime, with hot water only available in the showers from five to seven in the evenings except on Sundays, when there was none. Hot-water time coincided with supper which presented a dilemma. Wash and starve or eat and smell. The North Koreans were a further disincentive to cleanliness. There were three communal stalls, each with a single shower-head which could only supply enough water for two at a time, at the most. With the Chinese students, an element of unspoken 'after you' reigned. You damped yourself and your flannel and then retired to the side-lines to soap yourself, awaiting a turn to rinse off. The Chinese girls dried themselves vigorously with tiny damp towels. In defiance of practicality, the North Koreans bathed *en masse*, and there were twenty of them. Wearing identical plastic shower-caps to protect their bouffant hairstyles – 'We follow the hairstyle of Kim Il Sung's Beloved Mother' – they swamped the shower-room, pushing all others aside. They were tough and stocky, their solid figures perhaps also based upon the body-form of the Beloved Mother, so that even if you were covered in soap it was impossible to get near the trickle of water. It wasn't even possible to predict when they might storm the showers. Bathing was another form of guerrilla warfare for them and they preferred the surprise attack.

After the struggle to get into the University, it was something of an irritation to be told by the gentleman who gave us a formal welcome that this was not a university but a thermometer. The reason was that another poster campaign had started, running on so seamlessly from the Revolution in Education that the same posters were used, with little bits of paper with a new name on them pasted over the phrase 'persons in high positions pursuing the capitalist road'. Earlier hints were now spelled out: the erstwhile heir apparent Deng Xiaoping was being purged again (after a previous disgrace early in the Cultural Revolution). There were some new posters, too, which set out the Truly Awful capitalist things Deng Xiaoping had said like, 'An old fox is always a good fox' (a reference to political survivors like himself), or 'It doesn't matter whether the cat is black or white as long as it catches mice' (a shocking statement since it implied approval of feline expertise which was a Bad Thing: all cats should be simply red and their politics were more important than their skills); and he was accused of not paying enough attention to the three-in-one combination of old, middle-aged and young (being supposed to have said 'old-old-old', meaning me-me-me).

Being at the University raised our status in the diplomatic community, especially with the new poster campaign under-way. No one was allowed into the poster compound at the University without a student card. I spent all of my first

Friday afternoon there standing in the snow, jumping up and down to keep my feet warm and copying as many posters as I could because I had been invited to dinner at the Australian Embassy. Sure enough, though I was the most insignificant guest, I found myself seated to the right of the Ambassador. He wanted to hear all about the posters.

More restricted than we were, compelled to try and read between the lines of the *People's Daily* and other Party organs or to interpret briefings from the Foreign Ministry, diplomats were sometimes forced to resort to unreliable students to try and find out what was going on. Occasionally we found ourselves in possession of information we did not know we had. Sitting on a wall of a ruined Ming tomb in a quiet valley not far from the Great Wall, after a peaceful family picnic with the First Secretary, digesting caviare, pâté, wine and fruit, I remarked on the sudden changes in Gerry's room at the Institute. His room-mate, Di, was the son of a high-ranking army official and had recently been visited by his father who turned up in a giant black car with curtains at the windows and a military chauffeur. Gerry and Di had a washing-line strung up in the middle of the room and this was now adorned with a new set of pristine white underwear instead of the strange patchworks that no one would admit to owning.

The delivery of Di's new underwear turned out to be the last piece in an important jigsaw puzzle. Diplomats had been convinced that a high-level military meeting had recently been convened in Peking. They drove round and round the Great Hall of the People, the massive meeting hall on the west side of Tiananmen Square, looking for lighted windows and signs of banquets. They drove along the main streets, looking for army jeeps with provincial number-plates. Di's new underwear clinched the matter, for it transpired that his father was in charge of the military region adjoining Peking and that his sudden visit must have been connected with the meeting.

Similarly, large gatherings of people were watched closely in case they were about to hold a political meeting. On one occasion Colonel Greenwood drew the First Secretary to one side with a confidential air and whispered, 'I don't know if this is of any significance but I noticed a Large Crowd of

People in Dongdan yesterday afternoon . . .'. The First
Secretary nodded gravely and took note. He did not have the
heart to tell Colonel Greenwood that there was a cinema in
Dongdan.

I bought a geranium for my window-sill and a new alarm-
clock. I had hoped to get one with Red Guards waving little
red books on the second hand and lots of red flags on the
face but these had become unfashionable. As the violence of
the Cultural Revolution subsided into recent memory,
leaving only its institutions behind, consumer goods displayed a similar relaxation. I had to be content with a bright
blue clock that had a spray of plum blossom across the face,
depicted in silhouette like a paper-cut.

Owing to our late arrival in the history class which started
at the beginning and meant to get through to the end, we
missed Peking Man and the dawn of history and were
plunged straight into the Three Kingdoms (AD 220–80)
whose history of competing generals forms a great part of
Chinese folklore. At the fall of the Han dynasty, China was
effectively divided into three, with Cao Cao (son of the
adopted son of a eunuch) ruling the north, Liu Bei ruling
Sichuan in the west and Sun Quan the south. The campaign
to link Mao's former close comrade-in-arms Lin Biao with
Confucius, which had puzzled me in Tianjin railway station,
was an off-shoot of a longer-running historical campaign to
divide the whole of the past, including the Three Kingdoms,
into the Good and the Bad. I don't suppose that the Central
Committee of the Communist Party had read *1066 and All
That* but the similarities were uncanny. Confucius was the
original Bad Person because he supported emperors and
their divine right, oppressed women and encouraged the
working class to obey their rulers. The Good Guys were
the Legalists. This school, which originated with Xunzi,

held that human nature was irredeemably bad, whilst Confucianism, as developed by Mencius, saw humanity as fundamentally endowed with a moral sense. The Legalists believed that only through the imposition of laws and ferocious punishments could humanity be controlled and it was this philosophy, rather than any weedy stuff about good nature, that appealed to the Cultural Revolution leadership.

The first Qin Emperor, Shi Huangdi, who built the huge mausoleum with its buried terracotta armies outside Xi'an, was a Legalist and therefore a Good Thing. The Qin state imposed a series of standardizations, of coinage, script and the width of chariot axles, and promulgated laws, including an interesting one which determined the height (rather than the age) of legal responsibility. This persisted for two millennia, for on Peking buses there was a yard-high mark, indicating that you had to pay full fare if you were over a yard tall. We were not encouraged to speculate endlessly on the problem of juvenile criminals who suddenly grew a few inches whilst on remand. The first Qin Emperor presided over the mass destruction of Confucian works in the 'Burning of the Books' and had all the Confucian scholars buried alive. You cannot have too much of a Good Thing.

Cao Cao, who might have been considered a bandit anywhere else, was chosen to lead the Legalist team in the Three Kingdoms period. According to our lecturer, he applauded the rightful execution of his own brother, and his response to a Confucian who 'trumpeted nice clothes and old ways' was to 'impolitely put him to death'.

In history classes, we listened and took notes. In philosophy classes (we hadn't escaped entirely), we were divided into 'discussion groups' and our first discussion was announced to coincide with the appearance of Deng Xiaoping's name as the 'person in a position of high

authority who was taking the capitalist road'. It was difficult
to know quite how to comport oneself so we mostly fell
silent. The Chinese students were pretty silent too, but eventually they delivered themselves of little speeches of the sort
they presumably made at their own meetings, from which we
were excluded. Old Li, a soldier who slept ostentatiously
through all the history lectures, finally pronounced the name
of Deng Xiaoping which caused much nervous spitting and
clearing of throats. The Chinese students had obviously
been primed to regard all of us as spies and told to keep
things as anodyne as possible but an independent spirit
lurked beneath Old Li's sleepy exterior. I busied myself
during philosophy discussion classes by sweeping up all the
peanut shells on the floor (promoting hygiene). Everyone
ate peanuts during classes but nobody used waste-paper
baskets except for spitting into, when they weren't spitting
on the floor.

On Wednesday afternoons there was 'Culture'. In the first
session, we all learnt the smash-hit from the film *Rupture*, or
Split if you preferred: 'The pine trees on the mountain are
green, Control Revisionism; the bamboos on the mountain
are tall; Chairman Mao points the way, tralala tralala.' Beth
and I continued our own cultural explorations, biking into
the city to buy posters. The best was a pretty scene of the
origin of Chinese whispers, showing some soldiers knee-
deep in a lotus pond with huge pink blowsy lotus flowers
and great sea-green leaves getting in their way. They were all
holding their guns up out of the water and were apparently
whispering to each other, 'The enemy is up front, pass it on.'
There was also a snow scene, painted in a more active style,
which was dominated by a soldier lurching forward, his furry
army hat askew. Under the hat was a blood-soaked dressing,
the end of which trailed behind him. In the distance a group

of white-coated figures with red crosses on their caps were
gesturing wildly, obviously keen that he should come back,
let them finish the bandaging and perhaps indulge in bed-
rest to prevent further brain damage. But he was fearing
neither hardship nor death.

In a hardware shop in the Vegetable Market district, we
found some very good enamel mugs with pictures of the
Great Wall and the 'Friendship First, Competition Second'
slogan. Hardware shops were fascinating and I never passed
one without going in. They stocked straw mats, baskets,
bowls made of ceramic or enamel in all sizes, thermos flasks
and replacement parts, stove pipes and nails, and lots of
other bits and pieces. In the Vegetable Market, whose name
was synonymous with 'Go hang' because it was where public
executions used to take place, we also found some plastic
soap-dishes. An orange one had raised decorations on both
sides, one labelled 'Learn from Dazhai' with pictures of ter-
raced rice-fields, the other labelled 'Learn from Daqing' with
oil derricks. The best was bright green and bore the characters 'Deprivation and simplicity', words that were often
associated with Lei Feng who had only one pair of trousers
and whose socks were a nightmare of lumpy darning which
must have caused pedal havoc inside his army plimsolls. The
soap-dish lived up to its name because one side of it was
edged with teeth so that you could comb your hair as well, if
you didn't mind having soapy hair.

Foreign Affairs

Before lessons, there was a cleaning rota. Owing to the temporarily glorious nature of menial and dirty tasks, students competed to get up extra early to 'promote hygiene' in the classroom. This meant going in at seven in the morning and swilling water over the floor with an evil black mop. During lessons I preferred not to touch the desks because whenever a real hygienist had been in, they were all wet and horrible and made the exercise-books crinkle.

When I learnt that my Chinese room-mate was due to arrive, I promoted a positively scientific level of hygiene in our room. I also bought some paper narcissi bulbs in the Friendship Store and put them into a rectangular green celadon dish with a few carefully scrubbed stones, to join the geranium on the window-sill in welcome. Yang Huimei was twenty-five and had very pink cheeks. She worked as some sort of clerk in the transport administration but had been sent to the University to study world history, presumably to raise the class level of her filing. She was also learning English. I was shamefully glad that she lived in Peking and would therefore return home every Saturday afternoon, allowing me one morning to laze in bed.

We competed quietly in the promotion of hygiene, getting up at six to fetch a bucket of cold water and another evil-smelling black mop to swill dirty water over the floor. Yang Huimei told me that she and the other Chinese students had had a long series of lectures on sharing rooms with foreigners, mostly designed to put them right off the idea. Our loose morals, lazy ways and poisonously inaccurate ideas about everything were only compensated for by the fact that there were just two to a room in our dormitory, instead of ten, and, North Koreans notwithstanding, by the hot water available every evening downstairs, instead of in some distant washroom.

Yang Huimei had been taught that foreigners were unaccountably difficult about spitting. Chinese medicine holds that it is best to get rid of mucous as thoroughly as possible, but putting it on a cloth in your pocket was not regarded as a sanitary solution. In order to spare our feelings, Chinese room-mates did not spit on the floor of the room but opened the door and leaned out to hawk into the corridor.

I made my first visit to the University library. We had been set an essay on the subject of peasant uprisings at the end of the Sui dynasty and the efforts of the subsequent Tang dynasty to get landless peasants back to the fields. This was achieved through what was called a 'concessionary policy' by which the peasants were excused taxes for a few years in order to re-establish production, with the eventual aim of restoring the imperial coffers through agricultural taxes. Was this concessionary policy a good thing or a bad thing? Discuss. It was a rhetorical question since we all knew it must be a Bad Thing because the ruling class had thought it up and they were oppressive and only made concessions if they were advantageous to themselves. However, even to provide the required answer, I felt that some background reading was necessary. My first visit to the library was unsuccessful as they didn't lend books in the afternoons, only in the mornings. As we had classes all morning with only a ten-minute break for calisthenics, borrowing books meant going without lunch.

The library catalogues were the next hurdle. The Western-language catalogue was quite full but the Chinese catalogue drawers were almost empty since all the cards relating to books published before 1966 had been removed. Finding no references, I asked for an issue of the *Peking University Journal* published in 1956 which contained an article recommended by our lecturer. The library staff went into a huddle. Finally a representative emerged and asked me if a book would do instead? I supposed so and they found me two, both published pre-1966 and not listed in the catalogue but presumably approved in some grudging way.

At the beginning of March, it began to get warmer. It was wonderful to shed the padded jacket and rediscover free arm movements. Yang Huimei plugged herself in to her radio three times a day to listen to Radio Peking's English lessons, and the narcissi bulbs on the window-sill swelled and flowered. Outside it was sunny and blue-skied, and the newspaper headlines exhorted everyone to get out and plant crops. Yang Huimei put a jam-jar full of earth on the window-sill and began to cultivate garlic. The most exciting moment came when fresh young celery was served for lunch. Since November, we had had no vegetables except cabbage and the occasional onion. Throughout winter, Chinese cabbage was piled in dark corners everywhere: on the north-facing balconies of blocks of flats, in the street markets and on the pavements. The University's cabbage supply had been buried in a pit in the cold earth, to be dug up as required. I had never liked celery much but after four months of soggy white cabbage, its greenness and crispness were uplifting.

Spring affected the students in a predictable way. Keri arrived to join the philosophy class at the University, leaving behind a string of boyfriends at the Languages Institute. She immediately fell hopelessly in love with an Italian. The *grande horizontale* at the University was, however, a Romanian with a sulky pout. Mira had originally had a Chinese room-mate which considerably cramped her style. By a cunning combination of moves such as padlocking the door from the inside, leaving her poor room-mate jumping up and down in the corridor, or forgetting to padlock the door so that her room-mate burst in on a scene for which she had not been prepared, she had managed to get rid of her. With a room to herself, she cut a swathe through the foreign students. Mira was not interested in long sentimental attachments but prone to sudden switches of interest. One month, she would be seen everywhere hand-in-hand with a Canadian. The next, it would be a Yugoslav, the Canadian left red-eyed and visibly losing weight as he struggled with his emotions.

For a while, Mira consorted with a Cambodian student who called himself Dylan and played the guitar. He had been at Beida for a couple of years and was quite unlike the new Cambodian arrivals, sent by the murderous Pol Pot regime which had taken over since Dylan had left home. They wore Mao jackets over their sarongs and did everything together. Dylan had long hair, wore tight jeans and a leather jacket, and had nothing to do with the new student group.

Predictably, Mira tired of Dylan. He, however, refused to pine and starve but pursued her, arguing and pleading to be reinstated. I am sure that she did not think of the possible consequences of her action when she complained about him to her Embassy. She simply wanted to pursue her own life in her own way. But Dylan's fate was sealed. A week later, we stood open-mouthed as a large black car drove right into the University and stopped outside Building 25, the boys' dormitory. Grim Cambodian officials wearing long black coats gave Dylan fifteen minutes to pack and dragged him off in floods of tears.

We started contemporary history. The introductory lecture was given by a very fat man who lumbered into class looking like Yogi Bear in overalls. He carried a medicine bottle full of cold tea from which he refreshed himself constantly. The theme of the lecture (written up in yellow chalk on the blackboard) was 'What is contemporary history? How and why should we study it?' For over an hour it appeared that contemporary history consisted of dividing up the period between 1919 and 1976 into sub-sections and labelling them. But WHY do we study it? asked Yogi Bear. In order to comprehend fully that Chiang Kai-shek killed over 337,000 people in 1927 (he began to sob) and to learn how the famous writer and critic Lu Xun, wanting to support the Communists, sent them two hams. Here, in case we did not understand, he paused to write 'ham' on the board in English, mysteriously giving it a third tone, falling and rising, so that it was pronounced like Lady Bracknell's ha-a-a-andbag. Towards the end of the apparently interminable session, Yogi Bear recovered himself somewhat and proceeded to attack Western capitalist writers who wrote books THIS thick (he waved his arms contemptuously) but still failed to Grasp Essentials.

Monday, 4 March, was International (Working) Women's Day. We drew lots and I was selected to attend the celebrations as the English student representative. These celebrations took place in a mysterious grey building in the centre of town where women from all the embassies dressed in colourful national costumes mingled uncomfortably with officials from the Women's Federation in shapeless grey trouser-suits. There were performances of song and dance and the inevitable highly coloured tea party. At least I didn't have to give a solo rendering of 'Old MacDonald Had a Farm'.

After four frozen months, I had almost forgotten what

water looked like but, at last, the pools and ditches thawed and sparkled again. Spring was not all pleasant, however, for winds began to blow, whirling up dust-storms that darkened the sky for days. Walking to the canteen became a dangerous occupation as the wind raked through the rubbish piles and tossed used lavatory paper all over the campus. Lavatory paper was never put into the sewage system but placed in little wire waste-paper baskets. We were always being blamed for getting ill because we didn't wear enough clothes but no one had warned us about flying excrement. Rose and I sometimes amused ourselves by listing the interesting habits we could take home. Spit out all bones and gristle on the table at meal-times. Drop lavatory paper into any receptacle except the toilet bowl. When introduced, ask people exactly how much they are wearing and criticize their judgement. Another useful piece of medical knowledge that was imparted to us and which we longed to share was that cold sores were the result of a spider peeing on the rim of your enamel mug.

On 15 March, all heating in China was turned off for the summer. It snowed. I was taken to the Ming tombs by the First Secretary and his family, and we picnicked off asparagus tips and champagne. There were Jankowski's swans on the reservoir and sea-eagles trying to catch ducks. It surprised me how many Embassy staff were keen bird-watchers until they patiently explained that you could look at Other Things through binoculars whilst keeping up your bird-book as a front. There was shocking news about Dylan. He had been held in the Cambodian Embassy before being sent back to Phnom Penh but had escaped. He had turned up at the door of a foreign journalist and his wife in the nearby diplomatic compound. The Canadians had kindly offered him asylum but nobody could think of how to get him out of China in the face of Cambodian protests and the close links between Peking and Phnom Penh.

A pro-Deng Xiaoping poster had been put up by some German Marxist-Leninist translators at the Peking Foreign Languages Press. There they worked on German editions of Chinese pamphlets. One, attacking the Italian film-maker Antonioni for making a critical documentary about China, was entitled 'Cheap Propaganda' and was sold for

6 pence. The Germans said that the Soviet Union was the number one threat in the world, much more dangerous than the decadent West, and they were in favour of all sorts of unholy alliances in order to combat the threat. The Chinese went along with this to some extent, though it meant they acquired some very odd bedfellows. At that moment they were preparing a huge billion-dollar loan for General Pinochet, just to annoy the pro-Allende Soviet Union.

A couple of days later Yang Huimei stayed in bed all morning as she had her period. I prepared her cups of warm Lacovo, 'a delicious malted drink guaranteed to cure debilitation', and read *Shirley*. The Chinese would have loved it, torn as they were between their picture of England as a country full of Luddites whose faces were ground flat by capitalist boots and their longing to emulate our 'advanced' factories. That afternoon as our compulsory 'cultural activity' we learnt the latest chartbuster called 'Class Struggle is the Key Link', another series of mixed metaphors, joining 'Under the Great Conditions of Overthrowing the Rightist Revisionist Wind on the Education Front'. It was mercifully short:

> The lessons of history cannot be forgot,
> Class struggle is the key link.
> Once you've grasped this link,
> You won't fear wind and waves;
> Hold fast to it
> And the revolutionary victory is assured.
> The song of the Cultural Revolution
> Echoes in all four directions;
> Never forget Chairman Mao's instructions,
> Class struggle is the key link.

At weekends, the corridors of the girls' dormitory were full of Korean ladies in curlers helping each other to maintain their puffed-up coiffures modelled on the Beloved Mother of Kim Il Sung. We heard that the Australians had been expelled from North Korea. No official explanation was forthcoming but it was said that an Australian diplomat had bought an ice-cream in the street and was later called to the Foreign Ministry where complaints were made about an unwarranted intrusion into the internal affairs of North Korea.

Most of the foreign students went to the Liu Ban, or Foreign Students' Office, to protest about the impending visit of Richard Nixon. The Liu Ban always seemed to empty whenever you needed to find someone to sign an urgent chitty. When you didn't want to see anyone it was full of cigarette smoke with about twenty people sitting around in their shirt-sleeves playing cards. This time we were expected and there was a full turn-out of gentlemen in neatly buttoned suits. Our cadres explained smoothly that Nixon was a great friend of China because he had, in 1971, recognized China. Watergate was dismissed as 'the sort of thing that went on all the time in capitalist countries'.

On Saturday evenings, we often joined the other English students from the Languages Institute and went out to eat. Eating was the only possible social activity. The cinema came to us and sent us to sleep anyway, and there was nothing else to do. There was an excellent shop in Haidian, the little village opposite the University, which offered nothing except pork dumplings, the best being *guotie*, which were half-steamed, half fried with crisp bottoms and soft tops. The Long March Restaurant was just opposite the south gate of the University and had a neon sign which was an unusual modern touch in the little village. You had to be quick there

if you ordered eggs and tomatoes because tomatoes were
still regarded as fruit in China and came liberally sprinkled
with white sugar.

One of my favourite dishes was *Mayi shang shu*, or Ants
Climbing Trees, transparent rice noodles with peppery
minced pork (the ants) which you could only get at the restaurant in Sidaokou (Crossroads No. 4) outside the main gate
of the Languages Institute. Menus were difficult to fathom,
particularly when a dish happened to be called Palace
Pork, Eight Precious Rice or Pockmarked Mother-in-law's
Beancurd. They were also difficult to read as they were
chalked up on blackboards and half the items were 'off' most
of the time. A fairly wide, classical vocabulary was essential
for translation purposes, though some names were simple
but misleading: 'fish-flavoured meat strips' were much nicer
than they sounded. In the Xidan market there was a brilliant
Muslim restaurant which, eschewing pork, made a speciality
of roast duck, every bit as good as in the famous duck restaurants in the centre of town and a great deal less expensive.
Once, quite by chance, we ordered a dish of fried duck liver,
crisp and light, and served with a pile of roughly ground salt
and black pepper. I never managed to order it again though
one awful evening I tried. I couldn't remember what the word
for liver was so I thought I'd draw one. As I didn't know
where ducks had their livers I drew a person and a human
liver. My diagram met with anxious incomprehension.

One problem with eating in restaurants was that we
tended to be segregated. There was often a side room where
honoured guests were placed and to which foreigners were
invariably directed. We wanted to eat with the masses, even if
it did mean listening to a chorus of spitting and ending up
with heaps of chewed bones on the table-top. But it was
often difficult to resist being pushed into the side room with

its inevitable painting of the guest-welcoming pine tree or into splendid isolation upstairs where it was always cold owing to the lack of company. There was an upstairs room at the Xidan Muslim restaurant and one evening, when the downstairs was visibly bursting, it was suggested that we go up. Waiting downstairs would have meant that Chinese diners might be hurried or shoved off their table in order to accommodate us so, with evident bad grace, we agreed. To our embarrassment, upstairs was just the same as downstairs, though not quite as full.

Another cultural activity was announced at the University: 'Under the Great Conditions of Overthrowing the Rightist Revisionist Wind on the Educational Front, we are proud to announce a performance by the Liaoning Provincial Acrobatic Troupe.' There was a programme in English listing some sinister activities such as Bowl-flitting with Foot Manoeuvres and Friendship Conveyed through Silver Balls. Maintaining Balance whilst Discarding Bricks from Benches sounded like a complicated variation on manual labour. The acrobats unicycled backwards round tiny tables, flicking (flitting) bowls and spoons with their feet on to a pile balanced on their own or each other's heads. I liked the grand finale when all the traffic rules were broken and the entire troupe arranged themselves in a wobbly pyramid on one bicycle.

In pursuit of labour history, our class visited the Peking locomotive factory, called the 2.7 Factory in memory of a famous strike started by railway workers on 7 February 1922 (the Chinese put the month first). We stood about in cold sheds, helpfully holding handfuls of rust-less screws whilst the real workers made engines, but we were allowed to sit in the driver's seat of a Peking diesel. The real (political) reason for going to the factory was to hear from veteran workers about the strike. The two veterans were in their late seventies, rather like Chelsea pensioners with pink cheeks, white moustaches, medals and flat caps. One told us about the strike, for three hours. Fortunately, the second one contented himself with sending his love to our workers and wishing us a grand revolutionary career on our return home.

Just as we were getting ready to leave, with much shuffling and spitting (by the Chelsea pensioners and our Chinese classmates), the door burst open and a very tall man with a stick lurched in, bellowing cheerfully, 'I'm late!' He was over ninety, completely deaf and consequently unmanageable, not that anyone would have dared to interrupt a revolutionary veteran. He sat down and beamed at us, sucked up a cup of tea and started his speech. With only two teeth, he was impossible to understand, and being stone deaf, he was impossible to stop.

We were, in consequence of this repetition of revolutionary history, rather late for the spaghetti-*fest* organized by the comrades from the Italian Maoist Vento del'Este group, whose propaganda team was led by Claudio, studying philosophy at the University and a *maestro di pasta* in what little spare time he had. Keri was keen to help, being hopelessly in love with Claudio. He managed very well on a series of small electric rings. These were absolutely forbidden by the management and there were endless searches, rather like drug raids, of all bedrooms by cadres from the Foreign Students' Office in pursuit of illegal cooking equipment.

Poor Dylan lost his fight for life in the 'free' world, and perhaps his battle for life itself. After two weeks in the journalist's flat, a period of unbearable strain for all concerned, it became apparent that there was no way of smuggling him out of the country to Canada. Strenuous diplomatic efforts were made, but to no avail.

My Poisonous Influence

Spring continued its fitful progress. One Thursday, as snow fell steadily, we spent all day outside doing manual labour, digging huge holes in which to plant tiny fir trees. The next day, I bicycled to the New Summer Palace in warm sunshine. Quite a few trees had begun to flower, with tiny pale pink blossoms sprouting on black twigs, and rowing-boats were out for hire on the enormous blue lake. I found a lizard amongst the violets and was able to identify it as *Eremias argus* 'Peters' with the help of *The Herpetology of North China*, by Boring, Liu and Chao (Peking, 1932), which I had bought in the East Wind Market in Wangfujing. I made a circular return home, riding south-east beside the canal that led from the New Summer Palace into town. Leaving my bike beside the road I walked along a track between the fields with their little plots of green, grass-like winter wheat, towards the pagoda of the Temple of Benevolence and Longevity which I had seen in the distance when we did our open-door schooling nearby. It was a carved brick structure, all that remained of a temple founded in 1576, and it had marvellous fleshy stucco guardian figures and brick-built eaves. I found a gravestone in a field, which was odd because Chinese graves were normally just mounds of earth like giant molehills. There was a cross on the stone but any other inscription had worn away.

The following day I had a phone-call, summoned by the concierge who bellowed up the stairwell. I hoped it might be an unannounced bearer of a huge parcel of exotic cheeses but it was a friend of a friend. Maggie Keswick was the charming daughter of Sir John Keswick of Jardine and Matheson and Sino-British Trade Council fame. I went to meet him and 'his party' in the Peking Hotel. Lord and Lady Cranbourne were there and asked me, 'What do you DO?' I couldn't think how to explain to the aristocracy that I was a worker-peasant-soldier student and that I was learning how to throw hand-grenades in order to promote world revolution so I said, 'Nothing.' Sir John presided over lunch, vigorously shaking a china teapot in which he had mixed a personal brew of Chinese sweet white wine and Chinese gin.

Maggie was writing a book on Chinese gardens so we went off to the University to borrow a bike for her and cycled to the Old Summer Palace to inspect the ruins of the baroque buildings designed by the Jesuits where Maggie photographed the stone shell and some of the flower-draped columns. We moved on to the New Summer Palace where we started to measure parts of the Garden of Harmonious Interest by pacing it out. Before the gloomy light disappeared completely, we wandered along the covered walk beside the lake where Maggie took photographs of the painted pictures on the beams. These were mostly flowers and landscapes but some were a bit baffling. One looked like acupuncture to me so we asked a passing pair of gentlemen. They said it was tattooing. I think it must have been a picture of Yue Fei, a Song dynasty general who had the four characters meaning 'Ultimate Loyalty to the State' tattooed on his back by his mother. The gentlemen asked if there was any tattooing in our country and we said it was mostly done on sailors. Then they wanted to know where we came from and I said, clearly, England. As we walked away I heard one of them say, 'They're Albanians, no doubt about it, definitely Albanians.'

This happened quite often. The majority of the Europeans in China at the time were indeed Albanians, owing to the great friendship between China and Enver Hoxha, the only European leader to have embraced Mao Zedong Thought. Nevertheless, it was faintly annoying to have long conversations with people and explain things clearly, only to be completely ignored.

Yang Huimei tried hard to understand and persisted with *English by Radio*. Daily she intoned useful everyday words and phrases like 'denounce', 'slave-owner' and 'hatred' as in 'to have a deep hatred for somebody'. The radio broadcast a lesson about a slave army dealing Heavy Blows to the slave-owners who included the well-known creep Confucius. 'What have you done this week in the movement to criticize Lin Biao and Confucius?' asked the presenter, in such a challenging tone that I dropped my pencil. 'I put up a wall-poster,' said the presenter to herself. Keri opened the door. 'Frances . . .' she began in a tragic tone of voice which suggested I should be sitting down with a cup of well-sugared tea, '. . . Lowry's dead.'* Radio Peking's English lesson ended on a comforting Uncle Mac line, 'Goodbye, comrades, everywhere.'

---

* The painter. This was sad news in a general sort of way but neither of us had any special connection with him.

I got Yang Huimei to eat half a bar of Bourneville chocolate which was very different from dry and dusty Chinese
chocolate. She asked me what it was made of and, having
spent much of my time at primary school learning about
cocoa beans, I was able to tell her. She did not look convinced. The British Embassy promised to supply us with
books about Britain so that we could answer difficult questions after lights out, like how many middle schools there
were in our country. Beth's room-mate responded to almost
any nugget of information with the sentence, 'You have
been deceived.' She told us the Russians were starving and
worse off than before the Revolution.

'Funny you should say that,' we replied, 'it's just what the
Russians say about China.'

'They have been deceived.'

I had another of the Albanian-type exchanges in the
Forbidden City. I had gone to look at an exhibition of
ancient Chinese bronzes and was somewhat loaded down
because I had discovered a hardware store that specialized in
bamboo *en route* and had acquired, amongst other things, two
bamboo practice swords for *taijijian*. A man came up and
asked, 'What are those?' though he must have known.

'They are practice swords for *taijijian*.'

'Why have you got them?'

'Because we do *taijijian* at the University.'

'Who are you?'

'I'm a foreign student, learning Chinese history at Peking
University.'

'Can you understand Chinese?' (The whole of this
exchange had taken place in Chinese.)

'Oh, hardly any.'

In early April, as Qingming, the traditional day for sweeping graves and making offerings to ancestors, approached,

wreaths commemorating everyone's ancestor, Zhou Enlai, began to pile up in Tiananmen Square, at first around the Monument to the People's Heroes near the centre but gradually spreading across the square. Crowds of people came to look at the wreaths, to attach little pieces of paper with commemorative poems to the hedges around the Qianmen gate to the south of the square and to read all the other poems and inscriptions. Small crowds gathered around people reading their poems or making speeches about Zhou Enlai,

rather as they do at Speaker's Corner. We went down on Sunday morning and wandered through the crowds who, despite the solemnity of the occasion, were all quite cheery and friendly.

That evening, the Embassy telephoned and told us not to go to the square. All the diplomats did, of course, and watched a riot take place as the police removed all the wreaths and beat up the crowd which was later condemned collectively in the newspapers as 'The Tiananmen Counter-revolutionaries'. Apparently one young man was dragged about wrapped in wire and practically flayed. When the diplomats asked why, the crowd explained, smiling, 'He's a Qinghua University student.' As all the most vicious and self-satisfied articles in the newspapers were written by propaganda teams from Qinghua University or Peking University, and as they failed to reflect anything that ordinary people might care about, the crowd's reaction was not very surprising.

On the following Tuesday, to restore order and make everyone feel better and, in theory, to mark out Mao's successor as Chairman of the Chinese Communist Party, Hua Guofeng was presented to the nation, accompanied by a recommendation from Mao: 'With you in charge, I'm at ease.' This was painted up everywhere, appearing on the main blocks in the University, too. All day long, and all night as well, drums and cymbals could be heard accompanying apparently endless parades of workers who had been ordered to march to Tiananmen Square and pledge their allegiance to Chairman Hua Guofeng. In contrast to the spontaneity of the wreaths and portraits of Zhou Enlai and the cheerfulness of the crowd, these demonstrations were choreographed and lifeless.

The Ambassador and his family came, at our invitation, to lunch at the Haidian restaurant. The Daimler was parked discreetly inside the University gates as it might have caused something of a stir in the little village street. Clearly visible on the playing-fields beyond my window was a mass meeting (one of millions of compulsory gatherings held that day to endorse the new Chairman and the new order) which none of us should really have known about. The Ambassador kindly pretended not to notice. As Beth and I enjoyed a lift back into town in the Daimler, we passed more of the gloomy demonstrators who were all from ministries and institutions that had put up lots of wreaths for Zhou Enlai and had been ordered to re-march.

I got back to find a note. 'Frances: I'll get up tomorrow morning Five o'clock. So I lead to useing your clock. Thank you very much, Yang.' I went out at a more reasonable hour to take photographs of the lovely crumbling shop-fronts of Haidian. Lots of little boys gathered. Interrogated, I explained that I was taking pictures of houses to show English people. While they busied themselves finding me bits of stucco and carved wooden flowers a fat lady on a bike asked me why I was taking pictures of broken-down pre-Liberation houses? I ought to be taking pictures of lovely new concrete blocks of flats. To placate her, I took a picture of a small concrete department store and my little boys soon found lots of lovely concrete for me. I walked back to the University with them. We passed their school at which they all groaned like mad and forbade me to photograph it. I told them what I was studying and one six-year-old referred to the University as 'Your Beida', for which he was severely cuffed and told it was theirs, not mine. I was only a guest.

Photography was always a delicate matter. We went to spend a week at another commune on the outskirts of Peking where we lived with peasant families. Washing was reduced to face and hands only in an enamel bowl in the courtyard with chickens pecking at the splashes, but sleeping on the brick bed, well-wrapped in our own bedclothes, was fun. Not being able to go back to Beida for the lavatory was not. Beth's insides solved the problem by seizing up for a week. It had never occurred to me that I might regard the doorless squatters at the University as comfortable, but by peasant standards they were positively luxurious. To one side of the courtyard was a pigsty on top of which lived the chickens. Behind the pigsty was an earthen hut with a maggot-filled pit. It was essential to undo trousers and roll up trouser-legs well away from the latrine and then rush in, trying not to look at the maggots and holding your breath for as long as humanly possible.

One of the French students took a photograph of the lavatory which resulted in a furious meeting with the Chinese students who screamed at her. The level of hatred was frightening. Beth tried to moderate by saying that we were trying to learn. 'NO YOU'RE NOT' was the screamed reply.

I escaped, with permission, to join my parents. They had come to China on a tour and were being taken to Shijiazhuang. I was so pleased at the prospect of seeing them that my delight communicated itself to the other passengers on the bus to the station, ending up with one lady taking a very different view from that held by our Chinese fellow-students: 'It's only language that makes us different.' Two nice little girls insisted on carrying my luggage into the railway station which was basically an excuse to ride on the escalator. This was crowded with small boys running up and down the wrong way and railway officials shouting that they were class enemies.

On the train, which was going far beyond Shijiazhuang to Chongqing in distant Sichuan province, lots of people offered hospitality to my entire family, painting pictures of their green province where 'Even in winter you can get fresh vegetables', an attractive thought after months of dis-interred cabbage. A little peasant girl came into the carriage and sat staring sadly out of the window. A patrolling police-man asked her lots of questions and at first she wouldn't answer. But then in a great tearful flood she said she was twenty-two and her husband worked in the north, but he had sent her packing and she was going back to her parents in Sichuan, leaving her two children behind.

My parents' fellow-tourists included an Irish priest in plain clothes who wrote all his notes on the back of raffle-tickets. They were all already rather worn out with 'brief introductions' and had learnt that they were anything but brief. Light relief was provided by a lecturer in Soviet politics from the London School of Economics who would wait until the hopeless interpreter had stumbled for the hundredth time through 'Under the Great Conditions of Overthrowing the Rightist Wind on the Educational Front . . .' or 'The Struggle Against the Right-Deviationist Counter-revolutionary Wind Has Won a Great Victory in Eradicating Deng Xiaoping's Poisonous Influence . . .' and say, with a charming smile, 'I'm so sorry, I didn't quite catch that. Would you mind awfully repeating it?' On the bus, he engaged the interpreter in conversation, always friendly and smiling as he asked, 'Do tell me why you think Stalin found it necessary to kill all members of Lenin's Politburo except himself?'

'Their world-view had changed.'

'I see . . . fascinating.'

I travelled back to Peking with the group and accompanied them on some of their visits until it became apparent that my influence was almost as poisonous as Deng Xiaoping's. There was a cheerful gentleman called Herbert, Assistant Town Clerk of Camden, who collected posters. Keen to acquire some Chinese examples, he asked my advice. I sent him off one lunch-time, with misgivings, to Xidan where I had bought my best posters. Bus-stops were only marked in Chinese characters so, with the help of a map, we counted off the number of stops he should travel on the No. 1 bus, where he should change to a northbound

trolleybus (No. 14) and where he should get off. He returned
in triumph, loaded with posters, and informed me proudly
that he could have caught a No. 10 or a No. 6 back.
Enthused by his experience of public transport, he
announced, within the interpreter's hearing, that he planned
a short trip on the Underground.

Peking's Underground was a sort of military secret at the
time, part of a complex underground city that had been constructed in case the Russians decided to launch a nuclear
attack on China. The citizenry could then descend about
twenty feet underground and find a whole working city
awaiting them, always assuming that this was a very small
nuclear attack indeed. The interpreter was horrified at the
thought of a foreign local government official penetrating
this secret bunker and, clearly very annoyed, announced that
a compulsory official trip on the Underground would take
place before the visit to the Historical Museum that afternoon.

The Underground was not very interesting. The stations
were clad in local marble, discreet beige stuff, with none of
the splendour of the Moscow Underground. We went one
stop and then came back to where we had started in order to
complete the afternoon's schedule with a delayed visit to the
Historical Museum.

Three friends, who were studying at Fudan University in
Shanghai, were in Peking that week on a spring trip. The
Historical Museum was, at the time, officially closed except
to organized groups. History was regarded as a very dangerous weapon which could not be allowed to fall into the
wrong hands. The Historical Museum was also in a state of
continuous upheaval as different historical figures were reas-
sessed. Captions had to be adjusted, verdicts reversed,
exhibits withdrawn and heroic oil-paintings replaced. I had

told Richard, Bev and Michael that my parents' group was going to the Museum at two o'clock and that I was sure (quite wrongly) that they could tag along with us.

Owing to the unscheduled Underground trip, we arrived late, to find Richard, Bev and Michael standing outside the gates looking mutinous. They had been refused entry and told that they could only get in if they provided a letter of permission from their university. The English tourists were uncomprehending. Why couldn't these nice young people come in with us? They were students, why couldn't they see a museum? The interpreter was furious with me but found herself forced to argue with the gate-keepers and, with very bad grace all round, Richard, Bev and Michael were allowed in.

The interpreter informed me that I could no longer accompany the group on their visits so my father, who was fed up with brief introductions, and I went for walks along the narrow Peking streets, looking at song-birds in cages and buying second-hand seal-stones with little lions and dogs carved on them. I borrowed bicycles and we cycled around the University and the Old Summer Palace, and my mother almost wept when she saw the washroom and lavatories. Herbert left me a copy of *Country Life* with the headline, 'Chichester: city on a knife-edge'.

Negative Teaching Material

A long the road that led south from the University, the willow trees turned yellow and then green as the leaves appeared and soon the road was covered in willow fluff as the seeds were scattered. My parents had brought out from England for Pippa, a fellow English student, a pair of gold sleepers because she had suddenly conceived a passion for pierced ears. Pippa had arrived in China wearing contact lenses but the Peking dust had soon made these uncomfortable and impractical. I had taken her to get some glasses in Wangfujing. As she was a near beginner in spoken Chinese, I had been very worried about how they would test her eyes. She wouldn't be able to read many characters. It turned out that Chinese opticians did not use characters or the alphabet. Instead they had a lot of Es, some facing forwards, some backwards, some upwards and some downwards. All Pippa had to do was point to show which way the E was lying. When we went to the clinic at the Institute to try to get her ears pierced she tortured a young doctor into performing the operation, but his hands shook so much he dropped the syringe and had to go and lie down. It took him an hour to do it, trembling all the time at the thought of Red Guard interrogations: 'You indulged the disgusting bourgeois vanities of a foreign woman.'

As 1 May, International Labour Day, approached, all the vegetable stalls rearranged their spinach and cabbages to spell out the characters 5 and 1. There was a sports day at the University on 30 April. We were ordered to gather at ten past seven in the morning with our own little collapsible bamboo stools and line up in formation. We then had to march in ranks to the playing-field and sit in the sun for hours watching sports. Before any running took place there was a lot of parading and flag-waving. As they goose-stepped past with their coloured flags, the athletes shouted, 'Protect Chairman Mao! Long Live Chairman Mao! Develop Your Strength! Protect the Motherland!' I sat between Keri and a thin, bespectacled Chinese who said he was a first-year student of physics. This was a surprise as all the first-year students were supposed to be at one of the agricultural campuses, learning from the peasants. I asked him why he wasn't there and he blushed furiously and said he didn't know. Working on nuclear bombs, no doubt. As a great troupe of soldiers high-kicked past, Keri turned to me with her eyes shining and said, confidentially, 'You know I actually do think the PLA is the most wonderful army.'

Colonel Greenwood shared this view. 'Basically they operate on the same principle as we do. Officers and men are all friends and the officers muck in.' He revealed that there had been an awful lot of cheating in mock tank battles over Salisbury Plain until they introduced a cunning laser device which cut the ignition on contact and put a stop to the 'Got you!' – 'No, you didn't' – 'Did' – 'Didn't' that used to go on.

Keri took to smoking a brand of cigarettes called Red

Camellia and I begged packets from her to add to my collection of ice-lolly papers which was fast biodegrading. Ice lollies were sold by old-age pensioners in white medical uniforms from little carts where they kept the ice-lollies cool in thermos jars under enormous quilts. As it got hotter on the long bicycle ride into town, ice-lollies were the only way to slake your thirst. Eventually, I discovered one wine bar where, though it was full of sleazy drunks who spat and chewed on pigs' trotters, you could buy Shaoxing wine (a rice wine, rather like saké) if you brought your own bottle. However, it took weeks to discover a source of corks in a shop that sold medical equipment like trolleys and trusses; before that we had to keep a finger over the top of the bottle all the way home. It was surprising what you could do on a bicycle. I almost applied to join the Liaoning acrobatic troupe after cycling back from the canteen carrying two glasses of warm milk (with a saucer between them) for Sunday breakfast coffee.

On International Labour Day, we were bussed off, as usual, to the New Summer Palace. In the huge imperial opera theatre, we watched a dance performed by the Propaganda Team of Qinghua University. The theme was the unrepentant evil of those like Deng Xiaoping who had 'falsely repented' after the Cultural Revolution. Holding huge writing brushes the size of spears, the dancers stabbed at imaginary enemies, shouting 'Kill! Kill! Kill!'

In the centre of the city, all of the Ten Great Buildings were lit up with fairy lights along their walls, roofs and eaves, creating a dotted outline like Harrods at Christmas but multiplied by ten. They were so pretty we asked the Embassy bus-driver to go past them twice which he did, with much pride. That evening we sat in the New Summer Palace park watching bats flying low over the lake. The scent of lilacs was lovely, but it was hard to ignore the extra pink blossoms, made of lavatory paper, that had been wired to those bushes that had not flowered in time for the holiday.

I made progress with the library. Armed with chitties guaranteeing my urgent need to read bad books, I was issued with the works of Chen Duxiu, the first General Secretary of the Communist Party who became a Trotskyist and a fierce opponent of Mao. The books were stamped 'Negative Teaching Material' and 'To be Used in Criticism'. You could only get books by Zhou Yang, the main spokesman for culture and the arts until 1966, if you made it quite clear that you were aware of his position as a 'Counter-revolutionary Double-Dealer'. By now I was running out of things to borrow from the Embassy library, so I was delighted to discover that the Western language collections in the University library were unweeded and full of delightful reading matter composed by foreign counter-revolutionary double-dealers. I borrowed first editions of Henry James, once owned by a Peking resident with the interesting name of Mildred ffrench.

Yang Huimei went off to spend a month 'learning from the army', leaving me in charge of her garlic sprouts, and I had to get up early to see her off. Seeing people off was an important social duty and we spent much time hanging about beside buses carrying other people's rolls of bedding, thermos flasks, enamel basins and bulging string bags stuffed with bamboo stools and torches and other necessities of travel.

Though we didn't go to see them off, we did go to gape at the Languages Institute students on one of their 'open-door schooling' assignments. In an unexpected display of imagination, Tian Laoshi had arranged for them to spend a week in Wangfujing, Peking's Oxford Street, working as shop assistants or as waiters in the Muslim restaurant in the East Wind Market. Their arrival practically led to a week of riots. Wangfujing was not only Peking's main shopping street but also a magnet for all out-of-town visitors who came to admire the window displays of brightly coloured enamel wash-basins, dusty pyramids of beer bottles and little old-fashioned black-and-white televisions.

When word got about that Martians were serving on the apple stall in the No. 1 Department Store, crowds gathered.

There, Rose and Pippa, bright red with embarrassment, attempted to make a neat parcel of four large apples with a square of flimsy paper the size of a pocket handkerchief and a minimal piece of Chinese string. It was all strongly reminiscent of the cabbage and rice-straw problem. Chinese string then was made from twisted waste-paper and its tensile strength was exactly the same as that of rice-straw. In the pursuit of socialist thrift, the trainee shop-assistants were not encouraged to use a lot of string but were issued with inadequate pre-cut lengths. The paper, too, though brown, was flimsy like an aerogramme and rather smaller.

Sarah waitressed in the Muslim restaurant. She loved to creep up on a table of diners, surprise them with a polite enquiry as to whether they were ready to order and watch them fall off their stools. Ordering in a Chinese restaurant was normally a violent affair. Trying to keep the stool that you had fought for, you had to read the dimly chalked menu on a distant blackboard, locate a waitress and take her prisoner whilst she took your order. Sarah's willingness to please was distinctly unnerving.

Back at the University, a female teacher was rumoured to have supported Deng Xiaoping and put up anti-Mao posters. Amazingly, she was described as a rich landlord's daughter. 'And her name is Miss Scapegoat,' said the First Secretary. Quite how a rich landlord's daughter could have made her way into the University, normally reserved for politically correct workers, peasants and soldiers, was a puzzle but no doubt it was an evil plot of some sort. She was said to be touring the dormitories where she stood still for a long time while the inhabitants shouted 'Long Live the Revolution' at her. She didn't call on us but security was tighter than usual with lots of extra policemen stopping lots of vehicles in search of Bad Elements.

It was so hot that Beth and I cycled at geriatric pace to Weigongcun (the Village of the Duke of Wei), just south of the University, to look for the tomb of Qi Baishi, one of China's most famous modern painters who specialized in crabs, vegetables, shrimps and rats. I had already bought an enamel mug and wash-basin with his shrimps on them. I think we found it. Beside a block of flats, there was a clump of small stubby conifers surrounding a concrete stump. If it hadn't been for the cedars, we would have supposed the stump was something to do with the water supply. Tombs were rare since it had become a patriotic duty for modern Chinese to be cremated, thus saving agricultural land for agriculture. From the train you could see the earth mounds of ancient, traditional peasant graves clustered in the fields. One of the people on my parents' tour therefore assumed that people were buried where they dropped which conjured up a fearful picture of death in harness.

A break from the round of classes occurred with the visit to Peking of the British Minister of Education, Antony Crosland. He came to the University and we were summoned to the library. We stood waiting outside in the sun, chatting to the Vice-Chairman of the University Revolutionary Committee (the University's governing body) who was very friendly. He had a crew-cut. My mother had got very excited about crew-cuts since the counter-revolutionaries of Tiananmen Square involved in the commemoration of Zhou Enlai had been described as 'a handful sporting a crew-cut'. There were crew-cuts and crew-cuts, but the Vice-Chairman appeared to own his outright. A very short crew-cut was called a *pingtou*, or flat-head, whilst a completely shaven scalp was called a *guangtou*, or shiny head. The Institute's Mr Teazie-Weazie was unaccountably reluctant to perform a *guangtou* on Western heads. Perhaps he had aesthetics in mind.

Antony Crosland finally arrived in about twenty-five big black cars. The huge limousines with curtained windows used by important dignitaries were called Red Flag, just like the theoretical journal of the PLA and a very cheap brand of toothpaste. There were eighteen journalists on hand to cover the epoch-making event and the entourage included an Asian woman wearing narrow black wool trousers and a neat, distinctly fitted tweed jacket. She was something of a mystery, and because she was so well-dressed, I assumed she must be Japanese.

The Vice-Chairman of the Revolutionary Committee embarked upon a 'brief introduction' which was, of course, incredibly long and very badly translated. Crosland said later that he was very disappointed because he really was interested in education but had learned precisely nothing. He was also something of a joker because he asked, 'Could you tell me exactly what a capitalist-roader is in this context?' 'Someone who takes the capitalist road,' came the reply. When I told Keri about this afterwards, her eyes popped. 'He doesn't KNOW what a capitalist-roader is?' She was rather jealous of our brief meeting with the great man and had hoped to join in since her uncle was membership secretary of the Auckland Branch of the New Zealand Labour Party, but the University operated on strictly national lines.

We were pointed out as examples of foreign studentship. It was like being a model prisoner. The Ambassador's wife introduced me to the wife of the Foreign Minister, Qiao Guanhua, who was wearing the figure-hugging tweed jacket. She also had a chic, lightly permed hairstyle. Apparently the Australian Ambassador swore that she did her 'manual labour' in the hairdressers at the International Club (which was reserved for foreign diplomats). She chatted about open-door schooling but did not look as if she spent much time learning from the peasants herself.

As we trailed around the University in the great man's wake, we were shown into a room in the library that had up-to-date copies of *The Times* and *Time* and lots of other foreign magazines. This was simply amazing so I noted down the room number for future use. Needless to say, it was always locked and my enquiries about access were met with frozen silence.

In the evening, there was a reception at the Embassy. I wasn't allowed to shake the august hand again as I had already had my chance but I did meet Clare Hollingworth, the resident correspondent for the *Daily Telegraph*. She was great fun, with an amazing fund of stories from her eventful life covering the Berlin airlift, the Hungarian uprising and the civil war in Algeria, and was very generous to students, buying beer and *dandan* noodles (a spicy Sichuan dish) for us in great quantities at the International Club. She was very short-sighted indeed, with thick glasses, and was always asking Beth, 'Where is that beautiful fascinating girl?' Beth invariably replied that she hadn't the faintest idea who she meant and told me that it was a bit sad that my admirer should be quite so short-sighted. There were a lot of people from the BBC following the Minister, and the man in charge prefaced all his small talk with 'I can't give you a job.'

The next day I went for a walk in the afternoon along a road recommended by the Ambassador which was very pretty with some fine doorways. I found a heap of sand labelled 'Post Office Heap of Sand' but I couldn't find a post office. Back on the Educational Front, I was ploughing through *Feuerbach and the End of Classical German Philosophy* by Engels, in preparation for a 'discussion' in which everyone would say the right thing. I read it in English because that was sufficiently difficult to understand. It had been trans-lated in Moscow in 1949 and was full of capital letters. I did love Engels for his footnotes, though: '*see: The Nature of Human Brainwork Described by a Manual Worker.*' We were also instructed to prepare a speech attacking Chen Duxiu, who was credited with having invented Right-opportunism. Our teacher described him as 'wearing his right-opportunist hat'.

The ancient history class went on a visit to the Forbidden City to see the Ming porcelain. We got into one of the University's ancient buses which had no windows left and no padding in the seats. The bus parked at the north entrance of the Forbidden City, beside a small number of infinitely smarter tourist buses. Japanese and French tourists watched open-mouthed as we lined up in our philosophy discussion groups. On the order of our team leader, we numbered off and attempted to proceed in military fashion through the gate. I had problems with this, never remembering that you wheeled in the opposite direction to that in which you wanted to go. The French students also got in the way as they refused point-blank to co-operate: '*Mais c'est fasciste!*' With our battered bus, dirty Chinese clothes and shambolic attempts at military precision, the horrified tourists must have thought we were less-than-model prisoners from some special foreign gulag.

North Korean English

The largest groups of foreign students in China were the Albanians and the North Koreans. The Albanians were difficult to know, mainly because none of them spoke any English, and they kept themselves largely to themselves, although always in an enormous group. They had very odd names, often with an insufficiency of vowels. Their language was called Spyku or something. Teach yourself to Spyk Spyku.

The difficulty of communicating with Albanians reached a crisis in the summer. A British student called Craig* was unwisely swimming in the thick, green, snot-filled water of the Languages Institute pool. Beside the pool, other students were sunbathing. The sunbathers included Lucinda, an English student, very pretty with beautiful pale blonde hair. Her striking looks had attracted an Albanian athlete who was studying gymnastics at the nearby Physical Training Institute. He was tall and dark, with a wonderfully muscled body, and conversation was clearly not the foundation of the romance.

---

* Now Professor of Art History at the University of Sussex.

Craig made the mistake of looking down as he swam and his glasses fell off his nose into the impossibly murky water. Being very short-sighted, the loss of his glasses was a major disaster. Treading water over the spot and waving frantically, he shouted at Lucinda, herself no mean athlete, to come and help retrieve them. She leapt up but her Albanian boyfriend, misreading the situation, dived in and beat her to the spot where he started to wrestle Craig on to his back, in an attempt to save his life. Desperate to stay near his glasses, Craig struggled, both to free himself from the Albanian's muscular grip and to explain in beginner's Chinese, their only common language, that he was just looking for his glasses. The more he struggled, the more his rescuer fought to subdue him.

Unlike the Albanians, who did not seem to want to learn English to promote their revolution, many of the North Korean students had come to Peking for precisely that purpose. Though their equals in revolutionary fervour, the North Koreans could not have been more different from the Albanians. They all looked the same and every single one of them wore exactly the same clothes, all the time. The men wore badly cut Western suits and had uniform hair-cuts. The women had two outfits. For parties, they wore their traditional blue-and-white silk dresses. Otherwise, they wore the female equivalent of the Western suit, with thick orange stockings and sensible black court shoes. Male and female uniforms were finished off by covetable Kim Il Sung badges the size of saucers. These varied slightly but often incorporated fascinating features like suns behind the head of the Great Leader whose rays twinkled as the wearer moved.

At the University, the North Koreans were taught by an extraordinary old man who must have been in his eighties.

I first noticed him on a trip arranged for all the foreign students to the Great Wall, when he accompanied his troupe. He spoke English without a trace of a Chinese accent, fluently and beautifully, but with all the vocabulary of the 1920s. Good news was 'tip-top', North Korean male students were his 'dear boys' and the weather, on that day, was 'inclement'. He ignored the English students completely, probably regarding us as decadent in our use of language, betrayers of the style honed by P.G. Wodehouse and Bulldog Drummond. Jim, one of the English students, decided to supplement the old man's teaching by supplying the North Koreans with a few useful phrases but the teacher did not blink when his solemn, slightly thuggish students bade him a cheerful 'Pip-pip' at the end of the day.

The North Koreans were ferocious in their pursuit of linguistic excellence. It seemed that, as a nation, they would not take no for an answer. A German friend of mine called Tim wrote to say that, after an altercation over a taxi fare in Seoul, the taxi-driver called for help. A small Korean policeman got into the taxi. Tim, who was over six foot tall and well-built, decided to get out but the policeman fastened his teeth around his ankle and refused to let go. The same dogged persistence affected the North Korean students of English.

For some reason, I was selected as 'received pronunciation' star. A particularly persistent North Korean lady asked me to real aloud into her microphone. I assumed that this would be a single session of an hour or so, but I soon found myself locked into a throat-ruining relationship as she forced me to read through the entire Linguaphone course, day after day. This particular Linguaphone course must also have dated from the 1920s, and went some way to explaining their teacher's locution. The conversations mainly took place over tea, which was invariably brought in by the maid:

'Thank you, Mary, you may go now.' Ladies discussed the purchase of extravagant hats and their husbands chaffed them about the bills. Over pink gins, brought in by Mary who was soon sent back to her chores in the dingy kitchen, they creakingly joked about women's preoccupation with hats and men's enthusiasm for a bracing day on the links. It was no wonder the Koreans rabbited on about the slave class in the West. The obstacles to the promotion of international understanding were indeed manifold.

Occasionally, my Korean friend offered light relief in the form of Korean propaganda. We would sit side by side on her bed and look at the highly coloured and retouched photographs in books about the beauties of Korea and the wonders of its modern culture. There was one book with pictures of a Korean opera called *The Flower Girl*. It looked rather like *My Fair Lady* except that the heroine was called Ggot Bun. She had also ggot a long-suffering father. A book about the beauties of Pyongyang showed a nice lake near the capital, surrounded by azaleas which concealed 'hooting rabbits'. The caption to a photograph of soldiers crouching amongst the blooms stated that they were 'embosoming' the flowers.

I corrected essays at length. 'Kim Il Sung personally planted a pin tree symbolizing the military friendship between our two countries.' 'Ah! Bumper harvest! We shouted joyfully. Waving the ear of rice seemed to give us a warm welcome.' Or should it have read 'Waving, the ear of rice . . . ?' It was often difficult to tell. There was an absolute obsession with 'embosoming' and bosoms in general. 'The Chinese people are, indeed, leading a happy life in the bosom of Chairman Mao. With deeply understanding the women's life, we could see how the workers enjoyed themselves after working. The workers and we used to recreate ourselves with games.' There followed a touching description of my friend's happiness, despite losing a ping-pong match, because every time the ball fell to the ground, the workers would pick it up for her. She ended on an up-beat note: 'I am looking forward to having the second chance to go to the reality.'

I had intended to go on helping my Korean friend until she rewarded me with a Kim Il Sung badge. I really wanted one of the psychedelic ones where the sun's rays behind the Beloved Head moved if your bosom heaved sufficiently. But I terminated our relationship, in which I was beginning to feel a bit like Mary the maid, when she stamped a gecko to death during a lesson. It had been peacefully and helpfully hunting mosquitoes on the window-screen but made the mistake of overreaching itself and falling to the floor. I shall never forget the sight of the horrible court shoes in action.

Contrary to my expectations, a class discussion on the right-opportunist hat-wearer Chen Duxiu was quite fun. It

led to an argument about the disgraced military leader Lin
Biao and revolutionary procedure. Lin had apparently said
that the West was like the cities in China in the 1930s, and the
rest of the world was the countryside. Mao's line in the
1930s, after the Communist Party had been savagely
defeated when it tried to lead uprisings in the cities, and
despite the classic Marxist-Leninist premise that only the
urban proletariat could create a true revolution, was that revolution should be promoted in the countryside. This was
described (thin ice, thin ice) as 'developing Marxism-
Leninism'. Our group leader suggested that we criticize
Chen Duxiu who wanted to continue revolting in the cities
and also criticize Lin Biao for his remark. Lao Li, one of the
PLA soldiers in our group, protested that Lin Biao's view
was not so stupid. Our group leader said it was.

'Why?'

'Because everything Lin Biao said and did was stupid.'

'It wasn't.'

'It was.'

'It WASN'T.'

It was interesting that a soldier in his thirties should
defend his late leader because we often wondered how
people could love major political figures and then despise
them when required. Lin Biao's military career was currently
undergoing strenuous revision. Apparently the great strate-
gist had not been responsible for what we thought he had.

Discussing Feuerbach was more light-hearted. We wandered slightly off the point into Marxist dialectics which
Chairman Mao had helpfully summarized as 'One divides
into two – this is a universal phenomenon, and this is dialectics.' Serious discussion of this universal phenomenon broke
down somewhat when someone asked, 'Can a woman
change into a man?' The Chinese students fell to the ground

at the hilarity of this proposition. We decided to conceal the fact that it happened not infrequently in the Wicked West. A record of graduates in Chinese from Oxford University revealed that at least one had undergone a sex-change.

Arguments arose over summer clothing. It was oppressively hot. One of the French students, Cécile, decided to purchase some cheap white T-shirts. They were ordinary loose-fitting T-shirts, with a high neck and short sleeves, but they caused an absolute uproar. They were supposed to be men's vests and could only be worn by men and then only underneath a shirt, except in occasional sporting emergencies, and then only by men, too. No amount of philosophical discussion could dissuade Cécile. Nothing could appease our Chinese classmates. They explained how it was improper for women to wear sleeveless tops, however hot it was.

'Why?' demanded Cécile.

'Because women's upper arms are . . . ugly.'

'So why can't I wear these? They conceal my upper arms.'

There were two major aspects to the problem. There was the basic offence of a woman dressing as a man which would never do. Western journalists used to characterize Chinese clothing of the time as 'unisex' but it was far from it. Chinese women might wear baggy trousers in green or dark blue but they were women's trousers with a side fastening and no flies. They would never have dreamt of donning an apparently similar but subtly different pair of men's trousers. Chinese women might also wear baggy jackets in green or dark blue but they were women's jackets, without breast pockets.

Breasts were the second problem. Designating the upper arm as an area of 'ugliness' was a way of not referring to the adjacent breasts which were the real issue. Chinese men did not pronounce upon breasts in mixed company but Chinese women, in general, were against them. If they had any to speak of, they wore flattening liberty-bodices. Cécile had a fine figure but her room-mate made it clear that if she had had breasts like Cécile's she would have gone to any lengths to obliterate them.

Waists were also problematic. The Foreign Minister's wife in her fitted jacket had looked positively shocking to me after months of concealment. In winter, Chinese girls tucked their blouses into their trousers and pulled belts tightly around their waists. If it was warm indoors, they would take off their baggy jackets in the privacy of a room, but only in female company. If there was a knock on the door, it could not be opened until the concealing jacket had been retrieved and put on. In summer, girls wore blouses, which were not the same as men's shirts, though not wildly different, and they wore these over their trousers, to conceal any hint of a waist.

It wasn't only Western journalists who commented on the uniform clothing of the Chinese. Most visitors to China thought everyone looked the same, but this was not true. People did look different. There were subtle differences in dress for different ages, for example. The best thing to be in hot weather was old. Old gentlemen and even old ladies sat about in minimal vests and shorts, not in the least bit bothered about exposing themselves in their underwear. And beautiful people remained beautiful, despite their clothing. The female member of the PLA in our class, Gao Li, was tall, slim and extremely pretty, and she carried herself with incredible elegance. Her khaki army uniform could not conceal her natural beauty. It was interesting that she was a member of the PLA Propaganda Team (the singing and dancing troupe) and that she had clearly been chosen for her decorativeness. At the time, the official attitude to female beauty paralleled the official line on architecture enunciated in the 1950s by the brilliant architectural historian (and not-so-brilliant designer) Liang Sicheng, which was 'Utility, Economy and, if possible, Beauty'. Despite the official line, beauties like Gao Li rose easily through the ranks to positions of privilege.

We struggled to stay cool while at the same time offending the minimum number of people. It was impossible. One evening, as Rose and I cycled back from the Embassy, the heat broke in a welcome thunderstorm. This was only the second downpour we had seen since September, so we took off our jackets to enjoy the steamy subtropical rain. Huge white moths fluttered up to the occasional street-light and, as the rain weighed down their feathery wings, spiralled slowly downwards to the puddles. Cycling in the storm was a nightmare with lots of class enemies with no brakes skidding into each other. When Rose got back, her room-mate was appalled at the sight of her wet, clinging shirt. Yang Huimei was still away with the army learning how to use a bayonet so luckily there was no one to scold me.

Failing to Plant Rice

At a key moment in rice production, the history class was sent off to the University's agricultural campus near Fengtai, south of the city, where all students spent their first year. Before departure, I was taken aside as class-mother and told that 'If any of the girls want to, um, er, wear wellington boots, then that is all right.' I think I understood that menstruating women shouldn't spend time squatting up to their ankles in water, a health precaution that had been written into China's first constitution. Had I been told about rice snakes I would have taken wellington boots, delicate condition or no delicate condition.

Our first task was to gather young rice shoots and bundle them up, prior to transplanting in larger fields. The rice shoots looked like bright green strips of grass and were planted in little wet beds about two foot long and ten inches wide. The task was not difficult for the rice sprouts came up in handfuls from the thick mud. We washed the mud off their roots in the water in which they had grown and tied them up in little bundles with rice-straw.

It was not hard work, but it was back-breaking. Some

people had cunningly brought stools so that they could sit comfortably. The only problem with a stool was that it gradually sank deeper into the soft mud and lowered your bottom into the water with it. The best compromise was to sit on the bank of the paddy field and pick from there. The soft mud felt delicious between your toes until the conversation turned to snakes and leeches. There was a brief fight between two members of my philosophy group when Little Bao accused group-leader Old Bai of throwing a frog at her. He was a gentle person who wouldn't have dreamt of picking up a frog, much less of throwing it. The altercation led to much splashing and chucking of frogs and rice plants by the rest of us. Little Bao and Old Bai got on terribly well, enjoying the closest and best male-female friendship in the class. As they were both of marriageable age, it would have been lovely if they could have married. But, in classless China, Little Bao told us quite openly that she came from an intellectual family whilst Bai came from a peasant background, so marriage was unthinkable. Bai, who was a calm and tolerant man, seemed to accept this quite naturally.

At lunch-time we ate last year's rice, tangibly different, fresher and more scented than the usual gluey mess which was seven or eight years old. Then came real rice-planting. This was impossible. We tramped off to a huge water-filled field carrying our rice-straw bundles in baskets on carrying poles. It looked easy, separating the plants and poking them individually into the soft mud. But they just floated away. The only student who could manage it was not in our class. She came from southern China where planting rice was second nature. So we sat on the muddy banks and watched her.

The wheat harvest was no easier. We were bussed out to the wheatfields of a nearby commune and handed tiny sickles with curved blades. It was a boiling hot, humid day that called out for the relief of a thunderstorm. Bending double in the sultry heat hacking hopelessly at intractable wheat stalks, it became apparent that the only sharp bit of the sickle was the pointed end which I kept digging into my feet by mistake. With an appalling headache but pleading a more glorious foot injury, I was allowed to go and rest in a peasant house. I sat in the relative cool on a brick bed covered with a straw mat and played with a lovely baby. She was seven months old, wonderfully solid and cheerful, and was called 'Lotus of the Army'. Her mother slopped around in a vest as she was indoors, and breastfed the baby whenever she squeaked. Lotus of the Army had a tiny ginger kitten which was fed on scraps. There weren't many scraps and what there was was mostly *mantou* (steamed bread), but she seemed quite bright on her diet of dough. Lotus of the Army clasped her kitten in her fat arms and spent most of the afternoon laughing at me.

At the end of a not very productive day, we drank water in which sticks of sugar-cane floated and the leader of the commune discussed world politics. He was extremely distressed at Britain's dire economic position which he had read all about in the *People's Daily*. The *People's Daily* was occasionally very informative although it crowed rather about Britain's decline, the inevitable direction for capitalist countries. He worried that we might not get jobs when we returned. It was funny to have a man who earned practically nothing for his hard work being so sympathetic.

After *The Herpetology of North China*, I bought *Familiar Trees of Hopei* and discovered that the pretty tree with foxglove-like flowers outside my bedroom window was a catalpa and that there was a clump of gingkos beyond. The strange oak trees at the Ming tombs were Mongolian oaks. They looked like stage trees because their enormous oak leaves grew straight out of the trunks. The playing-field at the Languages Institute was surrounded by acacias which had begun to flower and smelled very sweet. The vegetable stores displayed spinach, large radishes, cauliflower, rape and garlic shoots. The latter were much stronger than garlic. I loved garlic, but I had to leave the room when Yang Huimei nibbled at the garlic shoots in her jam-jar. While she was learning from the army, they all died, I think through over-

watering. I was extremely nervous about this, but she forgave me.

We were ordered to go and watch a film called *Bright Sunny Skies*, about land reform, as 'historical material'. The landlords got their come-uppance but it took a long time and I was conscious of every passing minute. After the film, I rushed off to the pawn shop in Dongdan and bought some old men's gowns, as worn by landlords. The shop was in uproar as hundreds of Chinese fought over a consignment of second-hand Japanese jumpers that had just arrived. It was surprising that they didn't get an arm each, such was the scrimmage. Fortunately the landlord clothing corner was dark and quiet.

Rose and I made an intrepid expedition by country bus to Wanping, a small walled town beside the Marco Polo bridge, about fifteen miles from the city centre and just within the limit for unlicensed foreigners. The city disappeared in no time and we drove past green cornfields and through little villages. In one, Wulizhuang (Five Mile Village), the local carpenter had made marvellous window lattices, with the characters for happiness intertwined with the occasional five-pointed star if the window happened to belong to a family with a member in the army.

The Marco Polo bridge, known to the Chinese as the Lugou bridge, was so-called by foreigners as it, or something not very like it, had been described in *The Description of the World*, attributed to Polo. The bridge was long and low, with a series of elegant arches over the broad, stony river-bed, and it had little lions on top of all the balusters and two lovely stone elephants nudging either end. Beside it, the grey wall surrounding the village of Wanping, about twenty feet high and maybe a couple of miles in circumference, was still intact. We climbed up beside one of the gates and found that the top was about eight feet wide so we walked all around it, quite unobserved, which was strangely pleasant.

We looked down into courtyards below that were full of chickens and washing. There were more houses with delicate window lattices and geraniums on the sills beside pairs of newly washed cloth shoes drying in the sunshine. The chimneys were fun, too, with little flocks of clay doves along the eaves of the small pavilions that covered them. There were only two drawbacks to an otherwise peaceful Sunday. All the tannoys were set up on the wall, so we were treated to a deafening dramatized account of Deng Xiaoping's apparently endless crimes. And as we ate our picnic lunch we were terrorized by two goats with a passion for hard-boiled eggs.

In the University, classical Chinese classes provided occasional moments of pleasure, which was more than could be said for contemporary history or Marxism-Leninism-Mao Zedong Thought. We read two poems involving bird-song. In one by Li Bai (Li Po, 701–62), politically acceptable as it was written when he was exiled to Sichuan by the oppressive feudal regime, he wrote, 'Again, the night-jar calls, mournful in the empty mountains.' This was evocative enough as it stood but Chinese poetry is a complex thicket of allusion and apparently the night-jar's call is said to sound like '*Buru guiqu, buru guiqu*' which translates as 'Nothing is better than going home', reinforcing the despair of distant exile.

In another poem, Li Bai remembered his youth, spent fighting barbarians on China's borders, and the sadness of death far away from home. According to traditional Chinese belief, the spirits of the dead needed to be cared for by their relatives, hence the annual festivals of the past like Qingming in early April, when families gathered to sweep the graves, report to their dead ancestors and give them offerings of food. The spirits of soldiers whose bodies were left on distant battlefields were condemned to wander, eternally unhappy and hungry.

> The green mountains cannot repress my thoughts,
> Flowing east to the border,
> At evening on the Yangtze, I am sad.
> A partridge calls, deep in the mountains.

Partridges apparently say '*Xing bu de ye, gege*', or 'You won't get there, elder brother', meaning that Li Bai would not be able to go and care for the hungry spirits of his dead comrades-in-arms.

The small pleasure of unravelling Chinese poems was soon denied. We were told that classical Chinese would have to stop. I think the difficulty of finding enough acceptable passages was one reason but the overriding argument was that, owing to the recent 'reversal of verdicts', contemporary history was having to be substantially rewritten, and extra classes would be needed to make sure that we got right up to the present day with all the new lines clear before the end of term.

The final battles for liberation between 1945 and 1949 were a case in point. In our background reading material, which had been prepared in the autumn, the only two commanders of the People's Liberation Army who were still politically acceptable were Mao Zedong and Deng Xiaoping. Lin Biao was out, as were a lot of other famous generals. And now Deng Xiaoping had been rumbled, too. We were ordered to hand in our now-redundant and incor-rect background reading material and were given a special extra lecture by Lao Xu, the other PLA soldier in the class. This was four and a half hours long and terribly military, with incomprehensible maps that had great fat red arrows pointing one way and feeble white ones (for the Kuomintang and Chiang Kai-shek) pointing the other. Lao Xu was much better looking than Lao Li, with fine, sharp features and narrow eyes, so I did not much mind staring at him for hours. We were left with the distinct impression that had Deng Xiaoping remained in charge of the battle for Nanking, this major city would still be in Chiang Kai-shek's hands, rather like West Berlin. Fortunately,

Chairman Mao, now personally responsible for about a hundred different fronts (nominally in the hands of treacherous incompetents like Lin Biao) noticed the problem and rode to the rescue. Nanking was gloriously taken.

A Visiting Fireman

There were moments when we felt accepted. One lunchtime Keri and I went over the road to the Long March Restaurant and, after the usual ritual of refusing to allow sugar on the egg and tomato dish, settled down to eat. One of my classmates, Lao Zhang, came in with a girl and shyly asked if they could sit with us. Anywhere else in the world, this might have seemed a normal gesture, but not in China. Consorting with foreigners outside the gates of the University was dangerous. The Long March might be bursting with secret agents, ready to pounce on Lao Zhang and his girlfriend and interrogate them. I was used to being ignored by Chinese acquaintances if I met them in the middle of town. It was a bit hurtful but I wouldn't have wanted them to get into trouble. At a time when children were encouraged to report on their parents, and neighbours were urged to spy on each other, when it was considered everyone's patriotic duty to root out class enemies, merely saying hello to a foreigner in Wangfujing could be misinterpreted.

Even Keri, normally confident about her political credentials, occasionally gave way to gloom when it became apparent that she and her ideas were irrelevant and that there was little hope of any real friendships. I had read André Gide's account of his visit to Russia. There he found 'what visiting firemen always find' – 'intellectual apathy alternating with a superiority complex: a complete ignorance of the rest of the world and the conviction that Moscow is the only city on earth that possesses a subway'. The description was all too familiar.

Sometimes it was hard not to snap at people and develop a superiority complex of one's own. Yang Huimei didn't speak to me for a week after I told her that Tanzania was a member of the Commonwealth. In fact she was so outraged at the thought that a friendly African country with a nice new Chinese-built railway could be associated with the evil remnants of the British Empire that she consulted her world history teacher. He was reluctantly compelled to confirm my assertion and came round for an emollient visit which involved complicated exchanges along the lines of 'I know that you know, and you know that I know, but we must be careful how we present such information to Yang Huimei.'

The 'we know you know but kindly keep it to yourself' line arose often in class. During an interminable lecture on various class struggles in the 1930s, the teacher referred to 'the USSR, the first socialist country in the world under the great leadership of Comrade Stalin' and subsequently dismissed theories of 'human nature' as typically bourgeois fancies. Thomas the German, who knew his Marx, rose to his feet and said that Marx had discussed human nature at length in his early work. Undaunted, the teacher replied, 'I suggest you re-read your Marx, young man, and pay particular attention to *Feuerbach and the End of German Classical Philosophy*.' We had all read this, very recently, and knew it was by Engels anyway, but that didn't stop all the Chinese students from sniggering at Thomas.

Thomas was, however, impervious. Less than a week later, as the teacher listed all the accusations piled upon various now-disgraced leaders, Thomas rose to his feet again. If these gentlemen had indeed tried to make the Chinese Communist Party hand over all its guns to Chiang Kai-shek in 1945 at the end of the Anti-Japanese War, was this not because Stalin had ordered them to do so? What did he think

of Stalin's role here? The teacher coughed and spluttered and murmured that this was not, perhaps, Stalin's finest Chinese hour and should we not take a break now? In the break, he attempted to mollify Thomas by suggesting that they have a private talk about it very soon. This finally caused Thomas to despair because he knew all about it anyway and did not need the teacher to come round and discuss it and ask him PLEASE to keep quiet in class.

I had several of these 'private discussions' myself. In my essay on 'Concessionary policies at the end of the Sui and the beginning of the Tang', written despite the best efforts of the University library to thwart me, I had decided to argue that the policy was, indeed, of short-term benefit to the peasants. This was not particularly provocative since the essay was for the ancient history teacher Wu Laoshi's eyes only, unless he happened to decide it was so brilliant that it should be broadcast over the tannoy. With sorrow, Wu Laoshi tried to get me to accept the party line. I stood my ground but he was such a sweet man and I felt so sorry for him having to contort history into ridiculous positions that when we were set exactly the same topic with reference to the end of the Yuan dynasty and the beginning of the Ming (same policy, same problem, 650 years later), I wrote as he wished me to write.

One of Yang Huimei's English teachers came to ask me to record texts for him in my perfect received pronunciation. He picked up an ancient copy of *The Listener* which had a picture of Solzhenitsyn on the cover and lengthy transcripts of some of his articles inside. Though the Chinese were ferociously anti-Russian, it was only the post-Stalin Soviet Union that they disapproved of. The little man conveniently explained that Solzhenitsyn had been sent to Siberia in 1917 and had then left Russia, never to return until after the death of Stalin. It was therefore perfectly clear that Stalin could not possibly have been the object of Solzhenitsyn's criticisms.

It was usually foreign students who were accused of peddling such disinformation. I didn't listen to the World Service because to do so seemed to require the equipment of a radio ham but some of the students at the Languages Institute managed to find it and kept us informed. There was a difficult moment in May when Lee Kwan Yew, the President of Singapore, visited Chairman Mao. The World Service informed us that the interview had been so one-sided that it had been announced that Chairman Mao would give no further interviews. This news was dismissed crossly by Yang Huimei as capitalist propaganda but I had noticed that the television room was unusually crowded when the interview was broadcast. It was all very embarrassing. Chairman Mao was slumped in an arm-chair, with his niece and interpreter at his elbow. She was the Vice Foreign Minister whose hand we had shaken fairly frequently at state funerals. In similar interviews with visiting foreign dignitaries, it didn't much matter that Mao mumbled blindly because Wang Hairong 'interpreted' fluently and non-Chinese Presidents had no idea what the mumbles might have meant anyway. Lee Kwan Yew was Chinese and his bemused expression, as he strained to catch the mumbles, was revealing.

Chairman Mao did not appear on television again. As I bicycled past the huge concrete hoardings with his recent sayings painted on them in white on red, I wondered if they would replace 'Chairman Mao Says Never Forget the Class Struggle', 'Class Struggle is the Key Link' and 'Defeat Song Jiang's Capitulationism and Leap Over the Yangtze' with 'Chairman Mao says "Um, um"'.

Poor Yang Huimei. Fascinated by the similarities between Stalin and Chairman Mao, both of whom had ruthlessly eliminated all opposition, I asked her why Stalin had got rid of every single member of Lenin's Politburo except himself? She stuck firmly to the line that they had all died of disease, including Trotsky, though the ice-pick must have represented a complication. She refused to comment on the interesting fact that Stalin had also killed every single member of his own Politburo who was taller than him, and he was a very short man.

Whenever I felt particularly fed up about something, it was difficult not to take it out on Yang Huimei. The restrictions on travel for foreigners were particularly irritating. It wasn't just the endless chitties and travel permits and reporting to the railway police four times a day but the fact that much of China was simply closed. When we went to Wanping, Rose and I came up against one of the notices forbidding foreigners to move beyond that spot. On the way to the Great Wall, foreigners had to stop at a check-point and present papers. If we went as a group from the University, one of the Foreign Students' Office cadres had to walk up and down the windowless bus, collecting our little red plastic student cards for presentation at the check-point where every single one was examined minutely and at length. On the Wall itself, we were only allowed so far, before reaching a notice preventing us from proceeding further, written in Chinese, Russian and English and often accompanied by a soldier ready to enforce regulations.

Infuriated by the cordon, I demanded of the First Secretary at the British Embassy why we didn't put up signs in Hendon, Enfield, Bow, Deptford and Ealing, written in Chinese, Russian and English, forbidding foreigners from proceeding any further without written permission? And post soldiers to enforce them? He pointed out that this would not be seen as a punishment because such control was what all Chinese expected. In fact they were even more confined than we were, kept in their place by food coupons.

Sometimes Yang Huimei and I managed to have friendly chats after lights out. She was quite didactic, asking me what I thought about the latest *People's Daily* editorial? It had stated that cadres should not enjoy privileges (which they did) and that they ought to know more about their work. As I expressed general approval, and the pious hope that it might have some effect on the card-playing members of our Foreign Students' Office, we moved on to her experience of the Cultural Revolution.

'In my primary school, we criticized the leadership.'

'Why? Were they very bad?'

'No, they were fine.'

'So you didn't criticize them very severely?'

'Of course we did.'

I asked her if Liu Shaoqi, once Mao's heir-apparent but the major scapegoat in the Cultural Revolution, was still alive.

'I don't know and I don't care either way.'*

'But if he was alive you could see if he had changed his views.'

'He can't change his attitude; he's not like other people. He was a traitor. He betrayed his comrades before Liberation.'

She asked me if I wanted to get married. I mumbled something about there being no rush. She said that Chinese men were very keen to marry, though she didn't explain why. I think it was to do with its being the only possible access to sex. She must still think that Englishmen are cold fish because I told her that they were generally not keen on marriage. I also said that childcare was a problem in England. This she dismissed. 'You could give the children to your mother to look after.' As my mother worked, I pointed out that this might be difficult, but Yang Huimei, who had met

* His death in 1969 was not public knowledge at the time: details were only revealed after the downfall of the Gang of Four in late 1976.

my parents, had the solution. 'Your father is going to retire very soon, he could look after them.' I had a bizarre vision of my father as a Chinese Grandpa, squatting beside the North Circular Road with a lot of other grandfathers accompanied by bamboo prams with little children in them.

High Summer and a Third Funeral

The heat was relentless. As I bicycled lazily along at noon, heading for the New Summer Palace, the streets were quite deserted, the traffic lights turned off, the policemen asleep and the carters dozing on their vehicles beneath the willows. Even the frogs in the ditches beside the road were silent, sleeping amongst the pale blue water hyacinths. The Summer Palace was a haze of purple wisteria flowers. I wandered up to my favourite building, where the imperial family used to keep their caged birds and goldfish. It was a small pavilion built in the shape of a fan, with fan-shaped lattice windows and a platform in front with long stones laid out to look like a fan's ribs. Below it was a square pool. In high summer, the little fan pavilion had almost disappeared behind two huge clumps of sweet-smelling *Rosa banksiae*.

I often dragged myself out on my bike after lunch while Yang Huimei and the rest of the nation took a two-hour siesta. In Peking office workers went home for lunch and a long sleep, shop assistants cradled their heads on their arms at the deserted counters, and drivers stretched out in their vehicles. If I stayed in the room, reading quietly on my bed so as not to disturb Yang Huimei, I invariably fell asleep too and woke up at five feeling terribly bad-tempered. Some afternoons, led by Soren from Denmark who had a keen eye for intoxicants, Keri and I went out looking for cannabis plants which had sprung up along the verges of many roads. Our only competition for the plants came from flocks of fat-tailed sheep that grazed in the ditches by the side of the road as their shepherd slept under a tree.

Since it was too hot to work hard during the daytime, we were ordered to report for what was described as a whole night's manual labour, digging a huge hole to house the University's nuclear shelter. We lined up, numbered off, wheeled to the right and then to the left, and marched out heroically at eight in the evening, shovels over our shoulders, as the sun set dramatically behind the purple Western Hills. '*On dirait le Hitler Youth, quoi?*' muttered the French students. There were lovely stars overhead and a great sense of heroism as we dug until our hands blistered. At eleven the work was gloriously terminated and we marched off to a special midnight feast in the canteen where the kitchen staff seemed less than overflowing with gratitude for their shelter.

Another nocturnal excursion was arranged by the Embassy First Secretary who wanted to see dawn rise over the Great Wall. I arrived in some disarray as I had been asked out the night before by a friendly francophone African and the evening had not ended well. Under a fierce photograph of his own glorious leader, in military khaki with dark glasses and a thousand medals, he had announced that he had '*besoins physiologiques*'. I'd escaped but lost one of my gym-shoes as I fled.

Though it was not my normal practice to fulfil anyone's physiological needs after a couple of hours' acquaintance over dinner, I felt guilty about my lack of co-operation because Africans had a truly awful time in China. Students sent to study subjects like medicine were condemned to four or more years in a puritanical country where ebullience was regarded as a mental disorder and where there was widespread racial prejudice. They were stared at and talked about to a far greater degree than we were, and none of the comments were in any way favourable. When we were in Shijiazhuang, I'd noticed how the Chinese showing us round the Norman Bethune Memorial Hospital reeled back with unconcealed repugnance from the African students. Their body odour made some physically sick and there was no liberal conscience telling them to conceal their feelings.

Westerners were sometimes subject to the same blatant prejudice. White people are rarely put in that position but I can tell you that when it happens it hurts, terribly. To sense that someone finds you repellent because of how you look, because of your race, because of a physiology that you can do nothing about, makes you feel helplessly wounded. Later, it makes you feel incredibly angry and ready to hit out wildly. It is an impractical proposition, but I would recommend that white racists spend some years in a country like China so that they can feel what it is like to be on the receiving end. It deals a very profound lesson.

With me still feeling conscience-stricken, we set off for the Wall at three in the morning, driving carefully through the streets looking out for somnambulist cyclists in the dark. As we reached the country roads, our progress became erratic. At harvest time, the roads ceased to be roads and became threshing floors instead, with the wheat spread out over the tarmac to be threshed by passing vehicles. Little old men sat in temporary huts made of matting, guarding the crop against class enemies.

We also soon discovered that lorries used their headlights in a manner designed to create accidents. They drove fast with the headlights full on, but when they noticed another vehicle approaching, they turned them right off and disappeared. Then they flashed them on and off, on and off, until you were blinded and confused; and finally they turned on a little bicycle lamp placed in an odd position so that you couldn't tell where the vehicles were at all.

As we passed the police check-point where we should have stopped and shown our non-existent permit (foreigners were not allowed to go to the Wall in the hours of darkness), we crouched down in the car and the First Secretary accelerated. I think the policeman was asleep.

The Wall was dark and wreathed in mist. We sat on the cold stones, drinking coffee and sniffing the First Secretary's rum-sodden birthday cake when suddenly the sun appeared from nowhere. So did all the mountains that had been hiding, and more mountains to the west, and eventually bits of the Wall became visible with the mist being driven away at top speed across the green hills. All sorts of other things appeared. A mysterious thudding sound (a class enemy digging a shallow grave for another class enemy?) turned out to be a very old man cutting down a tree; a hare raced around like a lunatic, and tiny striped Siberian chipmunks charged up and down the Wall like squirrels on speed. Père David's Laughing Thrush (rare) laughed and a Chinese Babbler babbled. Rose, who was half asleep, said, 'There's that heckler again.'

By the time the first tourists, a noisy detachment of PLA men, appeared an hour later, all the birds and animals had disappeared. The Wall gradually woke up. The man who ran the children's corner took the matting off his equipment. He had a little tin aeroplane attached to a bicycle, a sort of primitive version of the Postman Pat machines you find outside supermarkets. With this particular machine, you put a child in the aeroplane and handed over a 2-fen coin. The man then pedalled furiously on his bike for a minute or two to make the aeroplane jiggle about.

A few days later Beth and I went on a romantic double-ticket to the Australian Ball. Unfortunately, owing to our University sleeping habits, the Ball had barely started before we fell asleep in two armchairs in the lobby. We missed all the fun but awoke in time for an early breakfast, making Marmite waffles on the First Secretary's waffle-iron with his children. It was rumoured that most of the guests were having their stomachs pumped out in the No. 1 Hospital and that one small Australian child had escaped from the flat and her sleeping *ayi* to find her mother emerging from the lift on her hands and knees.

As the wisteria blossom drooped, the swimming end of the lake at the New Summer Palace was closed to individual swimmers and filled with primary-school parties. They were ordered to celebrate the tenth anniversary of Chairman Mao's famous swim in the Yangtze. Rumoured to be old, ill and generally past it, the Chairman had suddenly emerged in August 1966, a head bobbing in the massive river, surrounded by solicitous members of the PLA swimming team. There was considerable speculation about the validity of the newspaper photographs – photo-montage techniques were suspected and the currents of the river at the spot were carefully analysed by the CIA.

As far as China's primary-school pupils were concerned, photo-montage or not, a Chairmanly swim was compulsory. Every swimming-pool, every available stretch of water in China was filled with skinny little children splashing about. At the Summer Palace, teachers in rowing boats bellowed at their charges, insisting that they swim with one clenched fist raised out of the water as a sign of extra determination. Most of them, poor swimmers at best, sank as they raised their fists. Fortunately, the water in the swimming area was only about three feet deep so mass drownings were avoided.

One hot day when I was climbing the stairs in the dormitory block, I heard the funeral dirge being broadcast over the tannoy. Someone had obviously died but it was hard to know

who. The music was always played *after* the solemn announcement, and since the tannoy blared all day long, nobody ever paid much attention. I went outside to find the paths filled with students standing still. Nobody quite liked to ask and nobody seemed to know. Finally, a Chinese whisper swept through the crowd of still figures and animation was restored. It was not, as we all feared, Chairman Mao but only Zhu De.

Poor Zhu De: despite his glorious and untarnished past as a general, his death was a tangible relief. Having heard him open the Third National Games just after we arrived, it was now our turn to buy him a wreath and get back to funeral duty. Mao's niece, Wang Hairong, and Chen Yonggui of the Dazhai production brigade, old friends by now, were solemn but not overcome. I was told later by a Chinese friend that amongst the crowds lining Changan Avenue to watch the cortège pass, there were more secret police than she had ever seen before. Perhaps they expected the sort of outbreak of mass hysteria that had followed Zhou Enlai's death.

I sometimes felt as if all crowds consisted entirely of disapproving secret police. It was wearing to be always in the wrong. It was tiring to be contradicted every time you opened your mouth. It was annoying to be told your clothes were unsuitable. There were times when I felt that I was never going to be embosomed. And though the Chinese students in our class always appeared to be right, there were undercurrents of tension even among them. A poster was put up by members of another class on a year's crash course organized for workers, peasants and soldiers. The class was called 'From Society to Society', but they seemed to feel that this meant 'Go back to where you belong'. Their poster complained that they were being discriminated against on two counts. When they returned from open-door schooling, it was 'without drums, without announcements' but they had been dragged out three times to 'warmly welcome' third-year students on their return from a similar stint. Then the swimming instructor, Zhu, a well-known prima-donna whose motto appeared to be, not 'Friendship First, Competition Second', but 'I WANT TO WIN', had refused to arrange a swimming class for them.

We had another major class discussion about Chinese history. It was a re-run of the question (expecting the answer NO) that we had discussed in relation to the establishment of the Tang dynasty: was the imperial government's temporary relaxation of its tax demands a concession to the peasants? This time, the question was exactly the same but related to the end of the Mongol Yuan dynasty and the establishment of the Ming dynasty in 1368. The historian Wu Han had published a biography of Zhu Yuanzhang, the founder of the Ming dynasty, in 1949, and there he had first enunciated the theory of 'concessionary' policies. Armed with a chitty from the teacher, I managed to borrow Wu Han's biography, clearly labelled 'Negative Teaching Material', from the library.

It was beautifully written and the most extraordinary story. Zhu Yuanzhang was born into abject poverty and his entire family was wiped out by 'famine and pestilence' in 1344. He then spent years as a mendicant Buddhist monk but eventually rose through the ranks of what amounted to bandit armies to become the first Emperor of the Ming dynasty in 1368. Not only did he promote these retrospectively much-criticized concessionary policies but he also set up free schools throughout the country in order to achieve a bureaucracy which would be truly *ouverte au talents*.

I stayed up all night reading Wu Han's elegant prose, and Yang Huimei stayed up all night reading it after me. There was, however, a major complication in Wu Han's historiography. For it was he who had later written the play about Hai Rui, the upright Ming official who had dared to criticize the Emperor. And it was the attack on that play, interpreted as indirect criticism of Chairman Mao in the long tradition of 'pointing at the mulberry and reviling the ash', that was generally acknowledged to have opened the Cultural

Revolution. Wu Han was therefore a very bad thing indeed. By the time we read his book, he had been dead for six years, dying as a result of beatings and medical neglect.

Even so, Wu Han had not suggested that Zhu Yuanzhang had anything more in mind than the re-establishment of agriculture for the benefit of the imperial coffers. We were told, however, that his theory implied that the ruling class had something to do with the means of production (the motive force of Marxist history) and that this simply could not be right. In our first meeting, in the small discussion group, I vainly attempted to defend him, guilty as usual of 'the foreigners' individualist approach'. It was like attempting to defend abortion to the Pope. The whole class then met, ostensibly to agree that such concessionary policies were not a good thing, but all of a sudden, Lao Li, the most ferocious of our PLA classmates, sprang a counter-attack and bellowed, 'There WERE benefits to the peasants.' He went on to shout down all opposition, thundering that he was not defending the indefensible Wu Han but that there *were benefits*. Not paying taxes was better than paying taxes. Little Li tried, subtly, to trick him, asking, 'If you were fishing and you caught a fish, could you say that the bait was of benefit to the fish?' I thought this was quite clever, though hardly a historical argument, but Lao Li stubbornly maintained his view. Arguments, especially with Lao Li, were vicious, as he shouted through everything.

Despite our being intimidated by Lao Li's fury, that discussion had been one in which the lines of battle were not drawn rigidly between Chinese and foreigners. Though I've no doubt that this temporary unity would have been short-lived, there was no chance to prove it either way. We reached the end of Chinese history with Hua Guofeng safely in charge and Chairman Mao at ease, and the class was about to disperse for ever for the summer holiday. Our Chinese class-mates prepared to return to their factories to raise the historical consciousness of their fellow-workers, and the Foreign Students' Office had been working hard on plans for the rest of us.

Holidays and Earthquakes

A huge treat was organized for all the foreign students in the form of a trip after term had ended in late July. The itinerary would take in the ancient capitals of Xi'an and Luoyang, Chen Yonggui's utterly revolutionary model agricultural brigade at Dazhai, and the town of Yan'an. There, in 1935, Chairman Mao had established his revolutionary government at the end of the Long March when the Communists had been driven out of their previous base in Jiangxi province by five encirclement campaigns launched by Chiang Kai-shek (who should have been resisting the Japanese invasion). Yan'an was the symbol of Communist resistance and, despite its remote location in the mountains, was visited by several American delegations during the Second World War, investigating Mao's mobilization of the local peasants against the Japanese.

Arrangements for our trip were made neither by post nor by phone since neither of these media were really trusted. The Post Office functioned reasonably well unless you were trying to send a parcel, in which case you were compelled to pack its contents in a wooden box and nail the lid down or, if they were soft, to sew them into a Post-Office-Preferred pillow-case in front of the interested gaze of all present and the friends they invited in for the show. The problem with the telephone was that it was regarded as a form of surprise attack. The standard Chinese answer to a phone call was not 'Good afternoon, this is the Peking Hotel, how may I help you?' but a snarled '*Ni nar?*' ('Who [the hell] are you?'). If you asked for someone who was not in, instead of offering to take a message or otherwise helping, the person at the other end would slam down the receiver with a fierce '*Bu zai!*' ('Out!'), leaving you precisely nowhere.

For these, and possibly other reasons (like a free trip for a large number of the Foreign Students' Office staff as a change from smoking and playing cards all day), all our travel arrangements were made by a group of teachers and cadres who undertook the whole trip in person first, to make sure there were no snags. There was not really much point in this practice run for the only unpredictable elements in the holiday were the foreign students themselves.

Keri and the Canadians literally danced for joy at the news that we were to visit Dazhai, but the prospect of three days in that hell-hole listening to recitations of highly unlikely and utterly unverifiable statistics with no possible retreat except to an unsavoury peasant latrine, filled the French students with deep Gallic gloom. Some of us expressed pious joy at the thought of visiting ancient capitals.

Our first stop was Luoyang in Henan province, the occasional capital of China from 206 BC to AD 917. We shared standard two-bed hotel rooms with the amazing luxury of a bathroom. After the North Korean showers, there was a huge temptation to soak in a bath all day. Hot water was plentiful, hissing and steaming out of the ancient taps, and even the lavatory worked fairly well, although familiarity with ballcocks and their foibles was useful. The hotel had previously housed a number of Russian technicians working in Luoyang's most famous factory which made tractors. Though they had been expelled in 1961 when China broke off relations with the Soviet Union, evidence of their stay survived. We were served strange local variants of Russian cakes, the best being a sort of seed-cake made with red bean paste instead of poppy seeds.

As a concession to Chinese history, we were driven to see a series of Buddhist caves and carvings. The Longmen caves were of a slightly later date than those of Yungang and many of the carved figures were less stiff and hieratic, more sinuous and Chinese. Since the river that flowed in front of the caves was in full spate, it was not possible to step very far back to admire the massive sculptures, as we had at Yungang. There, in mid-winter, the Buddhist figures had been dry and dusty and yellow, like the surrounding plain; at Luoyang, the stone was harder, dark with summer rain and overhung with greenery. We also descended into two stone tombs, damply dripping and with wall-paintings depicting a banquet and an expressionless lady hanging from a tree being nibbled by a tiger.

Driving out from Luoyang, past interesting villages with tall houses, their roofs steep and single-pitched, we went on to the Philosophy Commune where the peasants had applied Marxism-Leninism-Mao Zedong Thought to their agricultural efforts with apparently stunning results. Whether or not the application of philosophy had had any effect on their tomatoes, the application of a nasty chemical fertilizer certainly had. Their tomatoes multiplied endlessly. However, their efforts had almost been sabotaged by Lin Biao. They showed us a film about setting up the fertilizer plant in 1962 in which Lin Biao was represented by a thunderstorm through which they had to struggle like mad. The philosophical children did a dance for us. All the little girls were dressed up as butterflies in yellow full-skirted dresses with pale blue organdie wings. A fat little boy, supposed to represent Deng Xiaoping, was disguised as a hornet in yellow and black stripes and tried to sting all the butterflies.

During our brief visit it became apparent that the centre of Luoyang, which we were forbidden to visit, was full of posters criticizing the local Communist Party administration. As our time was fully occupied with bus trips which carefully avoided the centre of town, it was difficult to check them out. We proceeded to Xi'an in Shanxi province, where our cadres' careful preparations finally became apparent. Instead of decent rooms for two, we were herded into a vast disused ballroom in a hotel called the Renmin Da Xia (Great Mansion of the People). If you fiddled about with characters and tones you could easily make its name sound like the Great Prawn of the People. The ballroom was filled with hospital beds, and the showers brought back memories of the North Koreans.

Our cadres had made one huge mistake in choosing the Great Prawn: it was only a hundred yards or so from a vast square, just to the north-east of the city centre, and it wasn't far from Xi'an's massive old Bell Tower. The latter was, we noted with interest, plastered with posters. The square, too, had been taken over by an apparently popular bad element who called himself Liu Anquan or Security Liu. He had rigged up his own tannoy system and put up notices directing visitors to his dormitory 'amongst the trees'. Mr Security's tannoys broadcast constant crackling exhortations to 'Bombard the Headquarters'. When Chairman Mao had advocated this approach at the start of the Cultural Revolution he had meant that the Red Guards should challenge anyone in authority, all those ivory-towerists and unrepentant capitalist-roaders sitting comfortably in positions of power. Mr Security wanted the citizens of Xi'an to attack the Revolutionary Committee which ran the city.

The posters around the Bell Tower mostly focused on a local rape case, which made an exciting change from Deng Xiaoping and his gnomic pronouncements. They described a love-affair between two apprentices in a local factory. Apprentices were not allowed to fall in love until they had

finished their training, but the daughter of a highly placed local official and the son of more lowly parents had done so. They were apparently caught in a workshop doing something they should not have been doing when they should have been attending a political meeting. To avoid the shame of her collusion, the parents of the girl forced her to accuse her boyfriend of rape and the unfortunate youth was sentenced to three years in prison. All the poster-writers were

sympathetic towards the young couple and directed their
fury against her parents and their inappropriate use of personal power.

This attack on the local authorities provoked a mass of
further posters, written by local people with grudges against
the same authorities. These were small, personal and often
tragic. The Bell Tower was immensely attractive to all of us,
and to the Institute students who had only just arrived on
their own summer trip. Peking University and Languages
Institute cadres joined forces to mount patrols of the Bell
Tower and order us back to the Great Prawn, with little
success. Even if we agreed to return, it was still possible to
linger in the square and listen to Mr Security for there were
not enough cadres to cover both areas effectively.

Poster-reading was interrupted by news from the BBC
World Service of a massive earthquake, centred on
Tangshan, a mining town 45 miles north-east of Tianjin and
only about 90 miles from Peking. The earthquake had apparently also affected Tianjin and Peking quite severely. There
was, however, nothing about it in the Chinese newspapers.
Tian Laoshi from the Languages Institute found himself in
a difficult position. He desperately wanted to know if his
family in Peking was safe, but the only way he could find out
was through the BBC, the same medium that he had criticized so vehemently for its reports of Chairman Mao's
so-called interview with Lee Kwan Yew and similar bourgeois lies.

In fact, though Peking had felt the tremors there had been
virtually no casualties there. Nevertheless, the earthquake
made chaos of our carefully planned holiday. We were taken
off to Yan'an but had no idea what would happen after that.
We flew in a tiny and very old Russian plane. As we rose over
the city, white smoke poured into the cabin, provoking hys-

terical screams from the French students. I was sitting next to Edouard, one of Mira's French Canadian victims, who had been transformed through misery from a rather tubby person to a rake-thin depressive who also suffered badly from travel sickness. As he retched into his sick-bag, one of the stewardesses asked me if I would help her with her English. Glad to leave the sick-bay, we retired to the staff area and sat comfortably on little stools.

In those days aeroplanes in China were filled with loose attachments. Stewardesses would often bring their little stools out and sit on them during take-off. I always longed for a bump which would send them all somersaulting down the aisle like a circus act. There was, almost invariably, also a hat-stand, similarly unattached during take-off, landing and cruising. There was a famous story about the late lamented Zhou Enlai on a plane. The stewardess noticed a particularly old, battered and greasy trilby on the hat-stand. Holding it in front of her between pinched fingers she marched down the aisle and demanded, with an expression of disgust, to know who this filthy object belonged to. The late lamented Zhou Enlai acknowledged it as his and the entire planeload broke into sobs of admiration at his frugality.

'English for Air Stewardesses' was a battered booklet full of sentences like 'The sick-bags are in the seat-pocket in front of you. Please use them!' and 'Please hang up your hats and coats tidily on the hat-stand.' There was absolutely nothing about the white smoke that filled the plane on take-off. It was apparently quite normal and due to the design of the plane itself. I tried to teach the stewardess some helpful sentences to prevent panic but she couldn't see what the problem was so we went back to the sick-bags.

Yan'an was a small yellow-earth town set amongst dusty hills dominated by a pagoda which had become the town's emblem. Here, where Chairman Mao and some of his not-yet-disgraced comrades-in-arms had set up their revolutionary base area after the Long March, there were an awful lot of revolutionary sights to see.

On the first afternoon, we were driven out to the Date (or Jujube) Garden. There, the Communists had held open-air meetings by day and healthy ballroom dances by night. A pink-cheeked peasant girl gave us a brief introduction. As our feet went to sleep listening to her monologue, which was interrupted by heaving sobs every time she mentioned the late lamented Zhou Enlai, we looked around us. To my astonishment, there wasn't a date in sight: the entire area had been given over to marijuana with huge plants quivering in the breeze. Soren, never slow to react to such plant life, was surreptitiously plucking handfuls and stuffing them into his canvas shoulder bag.

We inspected the wonderful caves in which the leaders of the Communist Party had lived for ten years. They had been cut into a yellow-earth cliff and faced with marvellous decorative semi-circular lattice windows. Inside each there was a *kang* against the window and a small earthen stove beside it on which to cook. The stove also heated the *kang* in winter by means of a flue that ran underneath it. Owing to some oversight, Lin Biao's cave had not yet been reassigned. Most of his possessions in revolutionary museums elsewhere in China had been re-labelled. I'd seen Lin Biao's carrying-pole in Jinggangshan in 1971, only a month before he died mysteriously in a plane crash; Soren had visited Jinggangshan a couple of years later and the same carrying-pole was then said to have belonged to General Zhu De. When he mentioned its previous ownership, he was told sharply that it had always been Zhu De's carrying-pole. Lin Biao had stolen it.

Our guide wept copiously as she told us of the frugal life of the leaders in their caves. The late lamented Zhou Enlai had, as well as his disgusting hat, owned a (sob) 'three-uses overcoat', a dusty and much-patched Burberry still hanging on his cave hat-stand. He had used it as intended (use number one) and also as a (sob) blanket. I can't remember what the third use was now. The Yan'an Museum was full of similar 'revolutionary relics', including a vest which was so full of holes and patches that it was barely recognizable as a floor-cloth, let alone a vest. It had belonged to Dong Biwu, a founder-member of the Chinese Communist Party who had attended the San Francisco meeting in 1945 which set up the United Nations. There was also a stuffed white horse, allegedly once ridden by Chairman Mao. Soren could hardly contain his impatience during our visit to the Museum. He wanted to get back to the hotel and start frying his hash on the light-bulb for a pleasantly silly evening.

Our reverie was interrupted by the sound of sobs and screams from the corridor outside. It transpired that the Canadian students had been told that we would not, unfortunately, be able to visit the revolutionary production brigade of Dazhai, as promised, since the local airfield had been damaged by the earthquake. Their sorrow was uncontrolled but the sound of sobs was soon drowned out by cries of joy from the French students and other non-Canadians. Unable to travel to Dazhai, we flew back to Xi'an. We began to feel a bit like Peer Gynt, forced to travel endlessly with no hope of return to our mouldering possessions in damp, hot, earthquaked Peking.

The enforced return to Xi'an presented our cadres with something of a problem. They were unwilling to return to their Bell Tower patrol and so instigated a vicious programme of entertainment. There were compulsory visits arranged every day and compulsory swimming every evening. No excuses were allowed. I was very unwilling to swim in pools filled with spit and snot but was forced to don a black wool costume with three buttons on the shoulder and, scratching constantly, swim up and down, up and down, keeping my eyes closed and my mouth as far away as possible from the water. The swimming instructress borrowed for these compulsory sessions was inhuman. Her family was based in Tangshan, the epicentre of the earthquake that we still knew too little about, but she maintained an unearthly cool, ostensibly confident that the Party would take care of her relatives.

Compulsory coach trips took us further and further from the centre of the city. We were lucky to be taken to Princess Yongtai's tomb. A Tang princess, she was supposed to have been murdered on the orders of the only woman to reign in her own right, Empress Wu Zetian (AD 625–705). The walls of Yongtai's underground tomb chamber were decorated with murals and there were sets of funerary ceramics placed in niches in the walls of the ramp which descended to the tomb chamber.

We also went to the wonderful twin tumuli of the wicked Empress Wu and her husband, the Gaozong Emperor. The two great hills were linked by a 'spirit road' of massive stone winged horses and groups of tribute-bearing envoys, and just to the side of the spirit road were underground houses, square courtyards cut down into the yellow earth with tunnel chambers carved into each side, all faced with the same semi-circular lattice windows as we had seen in Yan'an. The winged horses were Tang in date but earlier funerary sculptures of the Han dynasty (206 BC–AD 220) stood beneath the funerary tumulus of General Huo Qubing (140–117 BC). These depicted tigers and horses, not quite free-standing but still struggling to free themselves from the huge boulders from which they were carved. Peasants were harvesting cotton beneath Huo Qubing's tumulus, stuffing the fluffy white balls into sacks on the backs of their bicycles, and the day we saw Gaozong's tomb, the green hills were misty and mysterious. In fact the whole plain was dotted with tumuli concealing the bodies of emperors, empresses, concubines, generals and high officials from the Han and Tang dynasties – a fine reminder of the power and wealth of those imperial reigns.

Unfortunately, we could not stay for ever. Our cadres informed us that it would be best if we left China as soon as possible after we were allowed to return to Peking. Any plans to travel through China on the way home would have to be abandoned because the earthquake had thrown all forms of transport into confusion. Nor would it be possible to stay in Hong Kong with friends: their small flats were already crammed with refugee diplomatic families. Those of us who would therefore be compelled to return by the Transsiberian Railway now had to get Russian, Mongolian and Polish visas for which we needed photographs. Uncertain about how well Peking was operating, our cadres made us appointments at a local photographer's studio.

I was sent off on my own to the photographic studio. I already felt quite familiar with Xi'an and, on local buses, had occasionally been asked, in a condescending sort of way, if I was 'one of our Xinjiang people' because in this north-western city, Central Asian Uighurs, with their lighter hair and Western features, were not unknown. When I arrived at the photographer's, I discovered that there was a queue outside. Though it was already after nine o'clock, the normal opening hour, the staff were still busy cleaning the windows and swilling down the pavements. I joined the queue and asked about the delay. 'They are promoting extra hygiene because an important foreign visitor is expected today.' 'Oh.' We waited. By ten-thirty, I had begun to wonder. At eleven, still unnoticed by the hygienic staff, I decided to approach the door and explained that I was from Peking University and that I had an appointment at nine.

To the embarrassment of the photographer, it transpired that I was indeed the important foreign visitor, but since I'd been standing outside, dressed in Chinese clothes, I'd passed for a local. They had been hoping for a blonde in a red ballgown with Minnie Mouse shoes and I was a huge disappointment. Clearly, I was already beginning to blend in. It was time to go home.

Aftershocks

By the time we were allowed to return, a fortnight after the great earthquake, Peking was still in chaos. There was no evidence of any damage but, as aftershocks continued, it was thought safer for people to move out of buildings in case they had been weakened and collapsed. Everything was operating out of its front garden. At the University and the Languages Institute, all students had been moved outside. Iron bedsteads draped with mosquito nets lined the paths, and students were only allowed into their rooms during daylight hours. Stray tremors, almost imperceptible, still shook the puddles and rustled leaves. My possessions were intact. Nothing had fallen off shelves or broken, although a pair of leather shoes, left in a suitcase beneath my bed, had grown an interesting green mould in the intense humidity. It had poured with rain for days after the earthquake, which was not much fun for the dispossessed survivors, sitting outside on their iron beds.

Earthquake stories abounded. An Ethiopian student at the Languages Institute, used to earthquakes in his own country, had leapt out of a third-floor window in the dormitory block and broken both legs. Had he been in Tangshan, this would have been appropriate behaviour. There buildings of three or four storeys reputedly sank into the ground; in Peking it was an overreaction. One of the madder Canadians thought the Russians had finally bombed Peking and her, and she went into hysterics. I particularly liked the story about Little Zhao, one of our prissiest classmates, who had apparently run straight out of the dormitory in her vest and knickers. Again, if Peking had been the epicentre, this would have been a wise move. As it was, most people took time to cover themselves decently and Little Zhao found herself virtually undressed amongst the crowd.

Gathering visas for the Transsiberian was complicated. Embassies might be operating out of their front gardens but it was still essential to acquire the visas in reverse order, each country wishing to be sure, above all else, earthquake or no earthquake, that it could get rid of me to the next. As all the embassies were on the far side of the city, we were allowed to stay over in the British Embassy whilst gathering the wherewithal to leave. Women and children had been evacuated to Hong Kong and the remaining diplomats were sleeping in their cars on the tennis courts, for fear that the Embassy building would collapse upon them. Jim and I were directed to the Ambassador's residence and offered sleeping bags on the floor. Before he retired to his car for the night, Colonel Greenwood made a final tour of inspection to check that we were sleeping in separate rooms.

I managed to acquire the visas but had trouble with money. I made a little extra by selling some things I did not want to take home through the Friendship Store. That particular section must have been responsible for the occasional appearance of Japanese jumpers when Japanese diplomatic families left for home. The disposal of my padded winter coat was watched with interest by the others. It was not practical to take it back to England where it rained in winter. The coat weighed a huge amount already. Waterlogged, it would have dragged me to my knees. However, it was in a fairly disgusting condition, with dusty footprints up the back and soy sauce down the front. Would I get more money for it if I had it dry-cleaned at the Friendship Store first? After going backwards and forwards between different departments and feigning ignorance of the coat's messy owner, I discovered that it was better value dirty.

The trouble with money was partly due to the extraordinarily rigid attitude of the Bank of China and partly due to the earthquake. Like every other organization, the Bank of China was working in its front garden and its employees showed no enthusiasm for entering the building to get me any Russian or East German currency, no matter how many visas and chitties I showed them. They maintained that an English person should have English money, no matter where they were going. With the pound sterling at a dizzyingly low ebb, I was compelled to travel for a week with only travellers' cheques (and no guarantee of being able to change them) and practically worthless pounds.

My luggage had expanded to a ridiculous degree. Unable to carry both suitcases myself, I invested in a bamboo pram, purchased for 20 yuan (about £5) in a favourite hardware shop in Dongdan, and had it transported back to the University in the Embassy minibus. When I experimented, it worked beautifully, taking both heavy suitcases with ease.

There were few farewells. Our Chinese classmates had all returned to their units and Yang Huimei was at home, sharing the difficulties of life in a front garden with her parents. I did not know where she lived. We had no end-of-term exams because Chairman Mao took a dim view of them. All I received was a 'certificate of attendance'.

My bamboo pram was a matter of huge embarrassment for Huang Laoshi, the cadre who had been appointed to see me off on the Wednesday train. It was clear that this was a last attempt to humiliate him. Wheeling a bamboo pram and followed by an assortment of foreigners, he was stared at by the thousands of people camping out in the parking area in front of Peking railway station with its pretty little pagoda roofs.

As Huang Laoshi got crosser and crosser with the curious crowds and the difficulty of heaving the pram on to the escalator, and as we heaved suitcases about the station in the thundery heat, my head began to ache. Keri wept. Frowning at her and smiling between clenched teeth for Huang Laoshi made my headache worse. I wanted them both to disappear. It was a relief when the train pulled out of the station. Its very movement sent a slight breeze through the carriage. I settled back against the unseasonal red plush seat.

The Transsiberian was blissful. It moved at a slow and stately pace across the Peking plain and through the hills, offering a fine view of the Great Wall near Qinglong qiao (Green Dragon Bridge). Beyond the Wall and its hills, the land grew flatter as we approached Mongolia. The transition from China to Mongolia was easy enough. I was uncomfortably conscious that I had a suitcase stuffed with class notes from the University which we were supposed to have handed in, particularly since they happened to contain praise for Deng Xiaoping, but the border guards just laughed hysterically at the bamboo pram and the assortment of straw hats that I had collected.

Mongolia was extraordinarily empty. Great plains of grass stretched to the horizon. After six hours of grass, there was suddenly a small man, wearing a brown silk robe with a bright pink sash, riding on a pony. He dismounted and stood beside the railway track holding up a yellow bat, some form of railwayman's signal. There didn't seem to be anywhere for him to have come from or to go to.

As the train moved slowly and steadily, it was possible to read comfortably on board. I also did some embroidery, making a wobbly cross-stitched sampler for my grandfather which read Home Sweet Potato (he was not amused). And I slept. The train was not crowded so Nina, a Danish student from the Languages Institute, and I had a compartment to ourselves. Even with the top two bunks taken up by our luggage and my pram we still had plenty of space to stretch out in.

Eating was more difficult. Beyond China, I had no useful money. At the Russian border, Nina and I attempted to change travellers' cheques. There was plenty of time, for the entire train had to be lifted off its wheels and put on to other ones since Russian and Chinese railway lines were of different gauges. The queue was endless, mainly because the two Russian ladies staffing the exchange were apparently working to rule. They looked up every single cheque in two huge volumes, licking their fingers, turning the pages, consulting each other, turning the cheques upside down, peering dubiously at watermarks. As Nina's money was being counted out, the engine-driver appeared and called a halt to the proceedings, regretting that he would have to depart now as we were already behind his schedule.

In the absence of cash I ate long-tailed anchovies from tins kindly donated by the First Secretary and otherwise borrowed from Nina. It was difficult to know when to eat anyway because we travelled through six time zones in four days, though the stations in Russia always showed Moscow time. The dining-car operated its own timetable and opened at whim. Sometimes we were able to walk down the train for coffee served in tall glasses with metal holders engraved with pictures of sputniks and heroic workers, or meat soup with bread and cheese, but more often we would have to walk back empty-handed as the dining-car was closed.

At Russian stations we leapt off the train and Nina bought little brown paper twists full of raspberries or a couple of carrots from the fat old ladies who sat on the platform. Getting off the train was worrying as I had heard of someone getting off and crossing the tracks to buy food, only to find a goods train rumbling by between him and his

train. Goods trains on the Transsiberian were miles long. By the time the thousandth bogey had rolled past, there was no sign of the Transsiberian. As Nina was my only source of money, I refused to let her cross any tracks and made her shop on our platform. On the last morning, we were all offered free fried eggs by the dining-car ladies who, over-excited by the thought of a few days in Moscow, decided to give away the remains of their larder.

In Moscow, we had to change train stations. I managed to load my pram and luggage, together with Nina's suitcases, into a Bolshoi (a long, station-wagon sort of car) and we were unloaded near the Finland Station. I urgently needed money to repay Nina before her train veered off to Denmark and I proceeded through Eastern Europe to England. Nina sat on all our luggage on a street corner as I tried to work out where there might be a bank. Neither of us knew the Cyrillic alphabet – I had excitedly informed Nina that most of the stations on the Transsiberian were called Pectopah until a German student explained that this meant 'Restaurant'. I'd been told there was a bank in Gorky Square. While I was trying to work out which signs might have the appropriate number of letters (and realizing that Lenin had exactly the same number, which wasn't going to help), a Rolls Royce drew up beside us. A fat, fair-haired man leaned out to ask if he could be of help. Any wariness I might normally have felt about white-slavers had disappeared after a year in Peking and I accepted a lift.

He had been intrigued by our strange garments – dark blue Sun Yat-sen jackets and unfashionably baggy trousers – and by the pile of luggage, but my story of living for a year in Peking with no night-clubs or entertainment was clearly so shocking that he took me to the bank, waited, and returned me to the street corner where Nina was still sitting patiently, so short-sighted that she was unaware of the crowds gathered about her.

From Moscow, the train ran through Poland and into East Germany at an unaccustomed speed. I shared a compartment with two nice ladies from East Berlin who fed me bread and sour cream and pickled cucumbers. They were travelling with a young man, the son of one of them, but as the train was organized by puritans, with men at one end and women at the other, he had to make a long trek to eat with his relatives. Volker, a German student from the Languages Institute on the same train, was frequently summoned from the men's end as I didn't know much German. My two nice ladies begged him to take care of me as they were sure that the East German border guards would make mincemeat of me and my pram.

East Berlin was quite scary, with jack-booted soldiers marching up and down the roof of the train. I had to change trains at the last station. Volker helped but I think the sight of the travelling circus was enough to make everyone leave us alone. As we drew into West Berlin, I felt, irrationally, that all would now be well. I was back amongst my own.

Though I half knew about the Berlin airlift, I had never really taken on board the fact that Berlin was still isolated. When we re-entered East Germany, I practically pulled the communication cord, convinced that I was going backwards. Volker explained, patiently, and paid for my ticket. In Peking we had been able to buy tickets as far as East Berlin for only £50, mainly because the Chinese had not spoken to the Russians since 1961 and had therefore not negotiated any price rise. By the time we got to Belgium, I was on my own. I offered some pounds to the conductor, who had no idea what they were worth (they were sinking daily at the time), and he waved them away. I did not have to pay anything else until I reached Dover where pounds were recognized.

On the ferry from Ostend to Dover, I stayed in the sun on deck beside my loaded bamboo pram. I was still wearing my baggy blue Chinese uniform and, without realizing it, was squatting in a position that had become comfortable over the year. I heard a group of English schoolgirls discussing me, confident that I could not understand a word. They could not imagine where I had come from, nor what I was.

Within a week, I had left China and crossed Mongolia, the Soviet Union and East Germany; I had left behind all that had become horribly familiar over a year and was returning to England with a bamboo pram and two suitcases stuffed with Simplicity and Frugality soap-dishes, an unrivalled collection of enamel mugs with slogans on them – 'Friendship First, Competition Second', 'In Agriculture Learn from Dazhai', 'A Single Spark Can Start a Forest Fire' (Lin Biao, no longer in production) and 'Serve the People' – a Lei Feng diary (with blank pages to record one's own simple heroism) and a number of vests with pictures of Nie Yonghui (yet another revolutionary hero) saving an express train and losing himself.

The bravest of the English schoolgirls approached and mutely offered me a sweet. 'Golly, that's very kind of you, thanks ever so much,' I said, sending her shrieking back to her friends.

Verdicts Reversed Again

It is difficult to convey how different England was after a year in revolutionary China. On my first morning back home, there was such an array of breakfast cereals (dreamt about, talked about) that I simply could not choose. Sitting on a bus, I began to feel vaguely paranoid and it took some time to realize why. The other passengers were taking absolutely no notice of me. I was used to being on buses where every single eye was turned in my direction and I was talked about, *sotto voce* and aloud. The silence and lack of interest on a London bus were unnerving.

Two weeks after I returned, on 9 September, Chairman Mao died. I went to write my name in the book of condolence at the Chinese Embassy in Portland Place. Despite my failure to be embosomed, despite the irritation of the constant attention and the occasional sense of real racial isolation, I still felt attached to China. After all the funeral duties I had performed, this was another. I felt as I would have felt in China, part of the mourning.

In the succeeding months, however, my natural cynicism returned. I went back to work in the library of the School of

Oriental and African Studies where I began cheerfully (and illegally) to put into practice some of the lessons I had learnt during my battles with the library at Peking University. Cataloguing a pamphlet written by Zhou Yang, the Minister of Education whom we had been encouraged to criticize during the early days of the Revolution in Education, I wrote on the title-page, in pencil, 'Counter-revolutionary Double-Dealer' because this was how I had been taught to think of him. Unfortunately, the pamphlet was subsequently bound and plasticized, and my pencil verdict conserved for posterity. I amused myself by (unfairly) classifying Taiwanese works of propaganda against China as 'Fiction'. But though Rose and I had planned to behave like Chinese on our return, we did not take up spitting in a big way, nor ask people how many layers they were wearing or drop lavatory paper freely.

On 21 October, it was announced that a 'Gang of Four' had been arrested two weeks earlier. Among them was Jiang Qing, Mao's wife. Two of her accomplices, Yao Wenyuan and Zhang Chunqiao, had risen through the cultural administration in Shanghai and had, together, led the attacks on Wu Han that had started the Cultural Revolution in 1965. The fourth was Wang Hongwen, a security guard from the No. 17 Cotton Mill in Shanghai who had mobilized his fellow cotton-workers during the Cultural Revolution.

While I was in China, there was no 'Gang of Four': these were a group of highly respected and feared individuals in positions of power. But as soon as they were arrested, wild rumours and accusations began to fly. There were revelations of the bizarre luxury of Jiang Qing's home life – her silk dresses (which in truth looked a bit like school uniform) and her photographs of roses with tear-drops of glycerin applied to the petals – which contrasted with her public appearances in military uniform brandishing a little red book. Was Wang Hongwen, 'self-assured' and 'photogenic', her lover? Had she thrown herself into the Cultural Revolution in order to purge artistic circles of everyone who had known her as a not very good small-time film actress in Shanghai thirty years earlier?

In November, idly cataloguing the latest periodicals to arrive from China, I noticed a correction slip inserted into the current issue of *Chinese Science*. It read 'In place of "the arch traitor and capitalist-roader Deng Xiaoping" read "Deng Xiaoping".'

Shorn of his epithets, Deng Xiaoping gradually returned to power. All the exercise books that I had filled with copies of posters attacking him were suddenly not quite the hot political items they had been when I'd returned, smuggling them past the Chinese customs. Now they were not worth the paper they were written on. All those hours spent standing in the snow copying out posters attacking Deng Xiaoping had been wasted. 'Open-door schooling' was abolished; exams for university entrance were reintroduced – no more worker-peasant-soldier students. My railway-engine making had been a waste of time. Bundling cabbage was retrospectively pointless, even while the citizens of Peking were still eating the cabbages I had bundled. It was no longer politically correct to plant rice far to the north of the Yangtze in defiance of nature, so all the rice plants that had floated away from me were vindicated. They were right to escape.

Over the succeeding decades, China changed dramatically. Deng Xiaoping announced that 'To be rich is glorious' and China embarked upon a rapid modernization, changing the face of the country I had known beyond recognition. Mao jackets were abandoned for mini-skirts, high heels and

Western suits. It seemed as if everyone in China, men included, had their hair permed. The hairdresser at the Languages Institute must have been working overtime. The country itself changed. The old Jesuit Observatory that had stood on the skyline at Jianguomen, with its astrolabes and globes silhouetted above the turrets of the tower, was dwarfed by skyscraper hotels. Tourists could now look down on what had once been Peking's skyline. Swathes of little grey courtyard houses were demolished and replaced by

faceless blocks of flats. The North Circular was superseded by three new ring-roads, and flyovers were constructed at all intersections, making Peking more of a problem for cyclists without gears. The systems of control and travel permits were relaxed, meaning that back-packers could reach areas of the country previously forbidden to foreigners but also that hordes of poverty-stricken peasants could flock to the cities in search of work on dangerous building sites.

And yet, however much they embraced the new China, nobody could really forget what they had lived through during what was no longer termed the Great Proletarian Cultural Revolution but 'the ten disastrous years'. When I visited the rare book section of the Peking Library in 1980, the incredibly old gentleman in charge introduced me to his assistant, a recruit from the mid-1970s. He asked if I could read 'the old characters' and, whilst I would not claim any great talent in that area, I admitted that I could. His admiration knew no bounds. Yet here he was, in charge of the national collection but still struggling to overcome a great gap in his education. That was one of the worst results of the Cultural Revolution. Ten years' worth of education had been ruined and, for almost all of those who had been through the 'educational system' at the time, there was no second chance.

When I took a tourist group down the Yangtze, one of the deck-hands singled me out and took me on to the front deck where, over the following days, he told me his life-story. He had not wanted to be a deck-hand but, because of the rigorous political investigation of potential students during the Cultural Revolution, he had been refused permission to go to university. He could tell me because I understood and I could not inform on him. Much as I longed for respite from his sad story, I had to listen.

Whenever I met Chinese officials, whether as members of visiting delegations to London or in China when I accompanied parliamentary delegations, the question of where I had learned Chinese invariably came up. The fact that I had been at Peking University in 1975–6 was an embarrassment to both sides. I knew that they knew that the courses then had been ridiculous, but none of us were to blame. We often ended up great friends. I can still remember the horrified faces of other diners as the top table, where the People's Association for Foreign Affairs was entertaining a parliamentary delegation from Great Britain, broke into song: 'We are going to build a university among the pine trees; the lessons of revolution cannot be forgotten; class struggle is the key link . . . tralala tralala'. I had learnt the song at Peking University, then and now the most prestigious university in China. The cadres singing with me may well have learnt the same song whilst 'learning from the peasants' under very different circumstances. Though years have now passed, there are still many in China whose lives were turned upside down, who saw much tragedy and who suffered. We cannot forget.

Even so, there are now several generations of young Chinese for whom the Cultural Revolution is only history. They giggle when I talk about it and report half-remembered reminiscences from their parents and grandparents. They have grown up under Deng Xiaoping's 'open-door policy' and do not know what 'open-door schooling' is. Though there are occasional half-hearted attempts to revive the cult of Lei Feng, his one pair of trousers must be a mystery to today's young shoppers who read fashion magazines and see Paris fashion shows on Chinese television and who would not dream of washing other people's underpants without asking.